D1232839

To Know St. Joseph

To Know St. Joseph

What Catholic Tradition Teaches
About the Man Who Raised God

MSGR. DOMINIQUE LE TOURNEAU

Catholic Answers Press

Published by
Catholic Answers, Inc.
2020 Gillespie Way
El Cajon, California 92020
619-387-7200
844-239-4952 orders
catholic.com

Printed in the United States of America

Originally published in French as *Tout savoir sur saint Joseph*
© 2020 Groupe Elidia Éditions
10 Rue Mercoeur
75011 Paris

Artège
9 Espace Méditerranée
66000 Perpignan
www.editionsartege.fr

Translated for Catholic Answers by James McMurtrie
Cover design by Theodore Schluenderfritz
Interior design by Claudine Mansour Design

978-1-68357-258-9
978-1-68357-259-6 Kindle
978-1-68357-260-2 ePub

Hail, Joseph, image of God the Father.
Hail, Joseph, father of God the son.
Hail, Joseph, temple of the Holy Spirit.
Hail, Joseph, beloved of the Blessed Trinity.
Hail, Joseph, faithful auxiliary of God's designs.
Hail, Joseph, spouse of the Virgin Mother.
Hail, Joseph, father of all the faithful.
Hail, Joseph, faithful to interior silence.
Hail, Joseph, friend of holy poverty.
Hail, Joseph, example of meekness and patience.
Hail, Joseph, mirror of humility and obedience.

You are blessed among all men, and blessed be
    your eyes, for all they have seen.
Blessed be your hands, which touched the
    Incarnate Word.
Blessed be your arms, which carried him who
    carries the world.
Blessed be your heart, burning with love for him.
Blessed be the eternal Father who chose you.
Blessed be the Son who loved you.
Blessed be the Holy Spirit who sanctified you.
Blessed forever be those who bless and love you.

Amen.

Table of Contents

Introduction

Mary is undoubtedly the exceptional figure in the history of humanity. She alone is the Immaculate Conception who was preserved from the stain of original sin in advance. This was done in order for her to become the mother in accordance with the flesh of Jesus Christ, the eternal Son of God the Father. Thanks to her, he became a real man, "as we are, yet without sin" (Heb. 4:15). This ensured our redemption.

But the head of the Holy Family that was formed in Bethlehem with the Savior's birth was not Mary. It was Joseph. This cannot be overlooked. If his role is discrete, it is far from being negligible. Consequently, we cannot separate Joseph from Mary.

I witnessed the following scene in December 1971, when the feast of Christmas was approaching. St. Josemaría Escrivá, the founder of Opus Dei, had asked that figurines be made out of baked clay for a manger that was under construction. When they were ready, they were brought over one day, wrapped in brown paper. The well-proportioned statuette of the Virgin Mary was the first one to be taken out and put on a table. Then, the statuette of St. Joseph came out. The one who was holding it in his hands placed it at some distance from the first one. St. Josemaría immediately reacted by saying, "Do not separate Mary from Joseph!"

In other words, put them beside each other in the manger. But also, let us not separate them in our interior lives.

It is in this mindset that we have undertaken the writing of this new book that is dedicated to St. Joseph. We hope that this will be a reference book about the holy patriarch as well as an opportunity to bring him out of the silence in which he shut himself away and that he sometimes continues to be wrapped in.

The first chapter, which is by far the longest one, follows the evangelical accounts of St. Matthew and St. Luke about Jesus Christ's childhood. It focuses on the person who was called to serve as Jesus' father on earth. It recounts known events—the marriage of Joseph and Mary, Mary's visitation to her cousin St. Elizabeth, the census that was ordered by Emperor Augustus, the Nativity in Bethlehem, the adoration of the shepherds, Jesus' circumcision, the arrival of the Magi, the flight into Egypt, the massacre of the innocents, and the finding of Jesus in the temple when he was twelve.

But this chapter also allows for the development of a number of other subjects. These include the origin and genealogy of St. Joseph, the annunciation of which he was the subject, his "doubts" when he observed that Mary was pregnant, the issue of Jesus' brothers and sisters, the nature of Joseph's being a father to Jesus and the heresies about the question of Jesus' siblings, Joseph's "silence," his vocation, his decision to keep being a virgin, his profession, his relationship to Mary, the care he provided to Jesus, his mission, his ordinary life in Nazareth, his distinctive dignity, the various patronages for which he is recognized; his age, death, burial, ascension, resurrection, and glory in heaven, and his connections to Jesus' passion.

It is easy to find "types" or foreshadowings of Joseph in the Old Testament. It is primarily the case with the patriarch Joseph, the son of Jacob, who was sold by his brothers and brought to Egypt as a slave. But other persons were related to him, such as Abraham, Jacob, Moses, and David, "the Lord's poor people"—up to John the Baptist, the Forerunner.

In passing, we mention some more recent people that Joseph has also been compared to, such as the apostles and St.

Joan of Arc. We also consider his superiority to the angels (chapter 2).

It is interesting to know what apocryphal writings say about St. Joseph. They say a lot about him and were often later taken up even by some Church Fathers. Chapter 3 gives us an overview of thirteen of these apocryphal writings by elaborating on the most important ones among them. It ends with some accounts regarding Islam and St. Joseph, the presence of which here is justified by the fact that the Quran was informed by some of these apocryphal accounts dealing with the subject.

The following chapter gives an authoritative foundation to the doctrine about St. Joseph and the veneration that is given him. It uses quotations of popes from St. Siricius in the fourth century to Pope Francis, and an overview of what the Second Vatican Council said about him. It is easy to note that the pontifical interventions became more frequent and abundant starting with Bl. Pius IX.

St. Joseph's holiness in general is the subject of chapter 5. It is understood that we must exclude the idea that Joseph was presanctified in his mother's womb. This is an aspect that, nonetheless, needs to be presented. St. Joseph's holiness is specified in various other aspects—immunity from lust, impeccability, and virginity. His relationship with the Holy Spirit and the most holy Trinity as well as the hypostatic union are considered afterward. Then we go on to his contemplation, his role as co-redemptor, his privileges and virtues: especially his faith, hope, charity, obedience, beauty, strength of soul, humility, purity, fidelity, prudence, patience, poverty, simplicity, and knowledge. This chapter ends with the way he sanctified his work and the nature of his prayer, which made him a teacher of the interior life.

Chapter 6, which is briefer, describes a number of the holy patriarch's apparitions. The most famous one took place in Cotignac, in the Var department.[1] These are distinctly more numerous than we usually imagine them to be. We also report on some miracles that are attributed to the holy patriarch's intercession.

Our study then logically continues to chapter 7 with an examination of the veneration of and devotion to St. Joseph, as they were progressively set up by different popes. The liturgy, with the Mass, prayers, and hymns that honor St. Joseph, take first place. Then, we go on to his function as the patron of a happy death and the patron of the universal Church. His role as an intercessor and his mission to sinners are expounded on before the major world sanctuaries that are dedicated to him are listed. (The most important one is the St. Joseph Oratory in Montreal.)

We have placed sidebars all along this book that offer additional information or clarifications, which are not incidental but are deemed to illustrate the main text.

Let us hope that the reader becomes enthusiastic about a discrete man on whom our Lord and the most holy Virgin Mary, and, in the final analysis, divine providence, could rely on to lead the Holy Family on its way in the world and support the divine plans as much as he had to.

Grenoble, March 19, 2020
Solemnity of St. Joseph

To Know St. Joseph

PART I

St. Joseph

in the

Gospels

Joseph's Genealogy

Joseph is a proper noun that comes from the Hebrew *Yosef* and means "he will increase," "he will add," or "he will offer growth." This patriarch is not mentioned very often in the Gospels. He essentially remains hidden. Yet he is presented as being the father of Jesus, the Savior.

St. Joseph's genealogy was organized by St. Matthew, who designated Matthan to be his grandfather and Jacob to be his father. According to Fr. J. Charbonnel,[2] he had two paternal aunts. One was named Sobe, who was St. Elizabeth's mother. The other one was called Anne, who was the Virgin Mary's mother. His oldest brother, Cleopas, had five children, namely: 1) St. Mary Salome, the mother of the apostles St. James the Great and St. John the Evangelist, 2) St. James the Less, an apostle and the first bishop of Jerusalem, 3) St. Joseph, nicknamed "the Just," who was a disciple of the Lord, 4) St. Jude the apostle, and 5) St. Simeon, the second bishop of Jerusalem, who was crucified when he was 120 years old.

Incidentally, we will notice the number of saints in Jesus' family. Charbonnel explains that Joseph was born in Nazareth, in the first year of the reign of Caesar Augustus. He adds that "in order to specify the date of his birth, we start from the tradition according to which the saint was forty years old when he married the Blessed Virgin. We also begin with the Roman Martyrology, which has our Lord being born in the forty-second year of Augustus's reign."

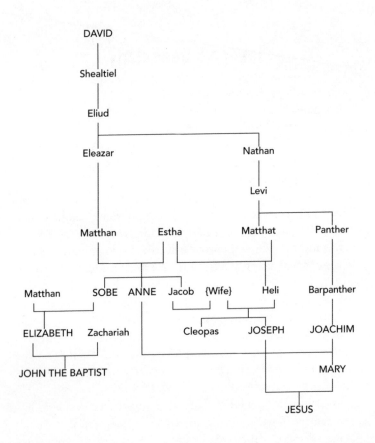

GOD WILL ADD

In Hebrew, *Joseph* means "God will add." God adds unsuspected dimensions to the holy life of those who accomplish his will—i.e., the important thing that gives value to everything, the divine. God *added*, if I may say so, the lives of the Virgin and Jesus our Lord to Joseph's humble and holy life. God is never outdone in generosity. Joseph could make the words of holy Mary, his spouse, his own. *The mighty one has done great things for me, for he has looked with favor on the lowliness of his servant.*[3]

In regard to Rachel's joy, we have written that "Joseph is a name of acknowledgement and desire. We sense what resonance this name must have had on the lips and in the heart of Mary when she gave it to her betrothed. Both of them wanted the coming of another one—the "desire of the nations." By pronouncing this name, Mary discerned a whole chapter of her people's emotion alongside a mysterious announcement of the future" (B. Martelet[4]).

At the same time, Joseph is descended from King David. That he was qualified to be from "the house of David" (Luke 1:27), "from the house and family of David" (Luke 2:4), "son of David" (Matt. 1:20), was very important for, according to the scriptures, "the Messiah is descended from David and comes from Bethlehem, the village where David lived" (John 7:42). As a result of an edict of Caesar Augustus "that all the world should be registered," everybody had to be registered in his hometown. This is why "Joseph also went from the town of Nazareth in Galilee to Judea, to the city of David called Bethlehem. It was because he was descended from the house and family of David" (Luke 2:4).

When the angel predicted to Mary that "the Lord would give the throne of his ancestor David" to the son that she had to give birth to" (Luke 1:32), he was suggesting that Jesus would be descended from David through Mary. He made Elizabeth depend on the priestly line by naming her as Mary's relative (Luke 1:36). But nothing prevented marriages between the descendants of the Davidic line and the priestly line. At any rate, Jesus could be enrolled in the Davidic line through his adoptive father since the line's legal status was determined by the legal father.

> Yes, Joseph truly was from the house of David. He really descended from a royal line. This man of noble race was even more noble in his heart! He was in every way a son of David and did not inherit any depraved person from his father David! Yes, he descended from his father in a straight line, less through his flesh than through his faith, holiness, and devotion. The Lord found him to be a man after his own heart—like another David. He very confidently entrusted the most intimate and sacred secrets of his heart to him.[5]

He is the man of both Testaments. "In his heart, he carried all the promises of the Covenant, with the assurance that everything was accomplished. He also had the joy of the New Covenant under his roof. Joseph, a man of God, was supported by the prophets. He had all the past for himself. His blood was that of the patriarchs. Having inherited their faith, he peacefully walked where God led him. Being firm in his hope, he never flinched. This firmness in the faith allowed the Virgin Mary to fill the role that God had entrusted to her" (B. Martelet).

JOSEPH'S AGE

The apocryphon called the *Story of Joseph the Carpenter* had Joseph die when he was 111, after he was with Jesus for about twenty years. Pierre d'Ailly (1351-1420) was the first one to talk about a young Joseph. Gerson (1363-1429) followed in his footsteps. Joseph was an active young man who was perfectly pure, eminently holy, and certainly sanctified, like John the Baptist in his mother's womb (see chapter 5). In the iconography, Joseph aged belatedly. The apparent old age in many of his ancient images, combined with the influence of the apocryphal writings, must have contributed quite a bit to persuading artists and poets in subsequent years of his advanced age. The reason for this aging is to be found in a negative image of chastity, which was considered to be impossible for a young man. This ignores Joseph's original holiness.

Mary's Husband

"Now the birth of Jesus the Messiah took place in this way. When his mother Mary had been betrothed to Joseph . . . an angel of the Lord appeared to him in a dream and said, 'Joseph, son of David, do not be afraid to take Mary as your wife'" (Matt. 1:18-20). We can ask ourselves:

> Perhaps this is the first time that David's fallen descendant heard himself be greeted with a royal title. The angel still thoughtfully and wisely awarded it to him. Joseph belonged to a royal race and was the son of David in anticipation of this hour. Joseph thought that it was the son of David that mattered then. Since he possessed the messianic promises, it

was necessary to learn that the prophecies were being accomplished. Because he had the royal rights
and privileges, we needed him to pass them on to
the most illustrious of all of David's sons (Fr. Buzy[6]).

Joseph was betrothed to Myriam or Mary of Nazareth.
According to St. Thomas Aquinas, this betrothal was appro-
priately done for Jesus and Mary and for men.

With regard to our Lord, this was appropriate so that
unbelievers would not reject him as an illegitimate child.
If the Jews and Herod had persecuted a child that was born
out of adultery, they would not thereby have acted repre-
hensibly. This also allowed for the compiling of Christ's
genealogy in a masculine line, according to the custom.
In this way, the newborn was protected from attacks that
the devil would have even more violently launched against
him. As St. Ignatius of Antioch noted, Mary was betrothed
"so that her childbirth would be hidden from the devil."[7]
Her betrothal with Joseph allowed her to escape the punishment that struck every adulterous woman. Thus, she
was protected from being dishonored, having been betrothed "to remove the infamous stigma of a lost virginity
from the one whose pregnancy would seem to have been
degrading," as St. Ambrose noted. In the final analysis, according to St. Jerome, it was "to show the help that Joseph
would bring her."

The betrothal of Mary and Joseph also suited us as well.
First of all, Joseph's testimony showed that Christ was born
of a virgin, for as St. Ambrose indicated once again, "Nobody testifies more authoritatively about the modesty of a
woman than her husband, who could feel and avenge the in-
sult if he had not recognized a mystery there." Then, Mary's
words confirmed her virginity and became more credible.
St. Thomas also found a symbol of the whole Church in

Mary who, "although virgin, was betrothed to Christ, a unique spouse," as St. Augustine wrote. Finally, St. Thomas says, marriage and virginity are honored in Mary "against the heretics who belittle one or the other."[8]

Joseph was "the husband of Mary, of whom Jesus was born, who is called the Messiah" (Matt. 1:16). The angel Gabriel was sent "to a virgin betrothed to a man whose name was Joseph, of the house of David (Luke 1:27). Since Emperor Augustus had ordered the whole world to be registered, Joseph went to Bethlehem "to be registered with Mary, to whom he was betrothed" (Luke 2:5).

According to these different texts, Mary is very much recognized as Joseph's wife, even if they did not yet live under the same roof when she welcomed the mission of St. Gabriel, who announced her upcoming divine motherhood. This was clearly inferred from the question that Mary asked the archangel right after this communication: "How can this be, since I do not know a man?" (Luke 1:34). The reasoning proceeds not so much from the first part, "how can this be," as from what follows—"since I do not know a man?" In other words: "since I am a virgin."

Because of Augustine, we agree to recognize a real marriage in this union, even if there was no sexual union and Jesus Christ's birth was due to the Holy Spirit's intervention. This was revealed to Joseph while he was sleeping: "Joseph, son of David, do not be afraid to take Mary as your wife, for the child conceived in her is from the Holy Spirit" (Matt. 1:20). The angel had declared to Mary, "The Holy Spirit will come upon you, and the power of the Most High will overshadow you; therefore the child to be born will be holy; he will be called Son of God" (Luke 1:35). If the angel "spoke to him so affectionately in a dream," St. Jerome writes, "it was to approve the justice of his silence."[9]

THE PROPHETS ANNOUNCED A VIRGIN BIRTH

St. Irenaeus wrote:

"From the height above or from the depth beneath" coincides perfectly with this other passage that says in regard to Christ, *"He who descended was the same also who ascended."* The phrase *"The Lord himself shall give you a sign"* highlights what is extraordinary about this birth. It was a miracle that could have been accomplished in no other way than by God the Lord of all, God himself giving a sign in the house of David. For what great thing or what sign should have been in this—that a young woman conceiving by a man should bring forth—a thing that happens to all women who produce offspring? But since an unlooked-for salvation was to be provided for men through the help of God, so also was the unlooked-for birth from a virgin accomplished; God giving this sign, but man not working it out.

On this account also, Daniel, foreseeing his advent, announced that a stone, cut without hands, came into this world. For this is what *"without hands"* means, that his coming into this world was not by the operation of human hands, that is, of those men who are accustomed to stone-cutting; that is, Joseph taking no part with regard to it, but Mary alone cooperating with the pre-arranged plan. For this stone from the earth derives existence from both the power and the wisdom of God.

Wherefore also Isaiah says: *"Thus says, the Lord, Behold, I deposit in the foundations of Zion a stone, precious, elect, the chief, the corner-one, to be had*

> *in honor."* So, then, we understand that his advent
> in human nature was not by the will of a man, but by
> the will of God.[10]

Starting with the benefits of marriage that Augustine identified, Thomas Aquinas saw a true marriage in the marriage of Mary, the mother of God the Son, with Joseph. This was because both had consented to a marital union, but "not a sexual union, unless God had wanted it." This is why the angel responded to Joseph's question by telling him, "Do not be afraid to take Mary as your wife." Augustine said that "she had been called a wife because of the first espousal, she who had not known and would never know of a carnal union."[11]

If this marriage was not consummated, the fact remains that the perfection relative to the education of the progeny was borne out in it. The bishop of Hippo informed us that "Christ's parents carried out all the goodness of marriage— the child, faithfulness, and the sacrament. We recognize the child in the Lord Jesus, faithfulness in that there was no adultery, and the sacrament in that there was no separation. The sexual union was the only thing that was missing."[12]

Peter Lombard (1096-1160) confirmed, along with St. Albert the Great (1193-c. 1206), that Joseph was not a father by accident because his marriage was ordained by God the Father to welcome and educate the child Jesus. Bossuet[13] confirmed that if a contract, sexual love, and children exist in each marriage,

> St. Augustine found these three things in St. Joseph's marriage. He showed us that everything contributed to guarding virginity. He found, first of all, the sacred contract by which they gave themselves

to each other. Here is where we must admire the triumph of purity in this marriage's truth. For Mary belonged to Joseph and Joseph belonged to the divine Mary to such an extent that their marriage was very real because they gave themselves to each other. But how did they do this? . . . They offered their virginity to each other, and they gave themselves a natural right by being virgins. What was this right? It was to keep it for each other. Yes, Mary was entitled to keep Joseph's virginity, and Joseph was entitled to keep Mary's virginity . . . Jesus, this blessed child, somehow came out of the virginal union of these two spouses. For, faithful ones, haven't we said that it was Mary's virginity that drew Jesus from heaven? Isn't Jesus this sacred flower that virginity grew? Isn't he the blessed fruit that virginity created?

This marriage's suitability was also supported by St. Bernard (1090-1153): "What man, seeing her pregnant without being married, would not look at her as a woman of ill repute rather than as a virgin? This could not be expressed in this way, at all costs, about the mother of the Lord. It was evidently better to think that Christ was the fruit of a legitimate union rather than the child of sin."[14]

MARY, THE NEW EVE

The Virgin Mary is found obedient, saying: *"Behold the handmaid of the Lord; be it done to me according to your word."* But Eve was disobedient; for she did not obey when as yet she was a virgin (for in Paradise, *"they were both naked, and were not ashamed,"* inasmuch as they, having been created a short time previously, had not first come to adult age, and then multiply from that time onward), having become disobedient, was made the cause of death, both to herself and to the entire human race; so also did Mary, having a man betrothed [to her], and being nevertheless a virgin, by yielding obedience, become the cause of salvation, both to herself and the whole human race.

And on this account does the Law term a woman betrothed to a man, the wife of him who had betrothed her, although she was as yet a virgin; thus indicating the back-reference from Mary to Eve, because what is joined together could not otherwise be put asunder than by inversion of the process by which these bonds of union had arisen; so that the former ties be cancelled by the latter, that the latter, may set the former again at liberty.[15]

Mary's Visitation to Her Cousin Elizabeth

"In those days," that is to say, as soon as she received the mission of St. Gabriel the archangel, "Mary set out and went with haste to a Judean town in the hill country, where she entered the house of Zechariah and greeted Elizabeth" (Luke 1:39-40). The village where they lived was identified as Ein Karem.

Elizabeth was a cousin of the Virgin Mary. The archangel had said to Mary, "And now, your relative Elizabeth in her old age has also conceived a son; and this is the sixth month for her who was said to be barren. For nothing will be impossible with God" (Luke 1:36-37). So, Mary made herself available for the last three months of her pregnancy. She "remained with Elizabeth for about three months and then returned to her home" (Luke 1:56).

For more than one author, Joseph accompanied Mary on this trip. This idea was found for the first time in St. Ephrem (d. 373). It entered into the devotion of the Latin church thanks to Gerson's (1363-1429) accounts about St. Joseph: "Was she alone on this trip? I cannot believe it. Even though the Gospel is silent on this point, I dare to assert that Joseph was there."

It seems completely plausible that Joseph did not want to let his young wife go on such a trip, which lasted for several days, by herself. Otherwise, we could have some doubts about his love for Mary.

This was also what Bernardino de Laredo (1482-1540) thought: "We must notice, if it is not written, that her very holy spouse accompanied her on this path. Nothing has been written that would prevent us from thinking that they went on this trip together. Joseph would not have been common-sensical or respectful in allowing the most holy Virgin Mary to go by herself. Her true honesty would not have increased in thinking he did not go with her." St. Josemaría also subscribed to this devout opinion.

When she left Ein Karem, Mary returned to Nazareth. Soon, the signs of her motherhood appeared. Her neighbors and Joseph her husband could not avoid seeing them. Joseph was deeply disturbed, as Matthew's account indicates (1:18-25). Let us carefully examine it, for the evangelist's conciseness has led many commentators to a false interpretation of the drama that was taking place in Joseph's soul.

ST. JOSEPH IN GERMANY

Leopold I, the emperor of Germany at the end of the seventeenth century, after having saved Buda from the Turks, was convinced that he had obtained a victory through the intercession of Mary and Joseph, whom he had called upon.

He asked for and got the Holy See to celebrate the solemn feast of the chaste covenant of both holy virgin spouses in his domains. From that moment on, the devotion to Mary and Joseph rapidly spread into all of Germany.

The most holy Virgin Mary's solemn introduction into her husband's home had not yet occurred because her condition had been noticed before both of them had started living together. They were still in their period of betrothal. Joseph was unaware of what had happened in Nazareth. Mary did not think it was appropriate to reveal her secret to him. She could rely on God to enlighten her spouse at the right time. She was "favored" (Luke 1:28). Her family inevitably knew her virtues. They did not need to be afraid of malice or slander. Her betrothal made her immune to all suspicion on the part of the anonymous crowd. But what could Joseph think?

As it so happens, a few Fathers of the Church, notably Augustine and St. Justin, advanced a real doubt about her. Matthew's text conflicts with this exegesis. He, in fact, wrote that "her husband Joseph, being a righteous man, was unwilling to expose her to public disgrace" (Matt. 1:19). By reason of his justness, Joseph could not have denounced Mary. Before a husband who was perfectly calm and who was so virtuous, Isaiah's reflection on the virgin mother (7:14) or the thought of a divine intervention must have presented itself to his soul. His obedience to the angel who appeared to him in a dream demonstrated this. But could he then agree to stay close to a virgin who was so favored by God and be a father to the child she would give birth to? According to his humility, he tended toward stepping aside: "He planned to dismiss her quietly" (Matt. 1:19).

Still unsure, Joseph was about to be fully instructed. An angel appeared to him in a dream whose message dispelled his anxiety. "Joseph, son of David, do not be afraid to take Mary as your wife, for the child conceived in her is from the Holy Spirit. She will bear a son, and you are to name him Jesus, for he will save his people from their sins" (Matt. 1:20–21).

Joseph's Annunciation

We can say that Joseph thus benefited from an annunciation that was parallel to the one that Mary received. "Now the birth of Jesus the Messiah took place in this way. When his mother Mary had been betrothed to Joseph, but before they lived together, she was found to be with child from the Holy Spirit. Her husband Joseph, being a righteous man, and unwilling to expose her to public disgrace, planned to dismiss her quietly" (Matt. 1:18–19). He had prepared this plan when the angel of the Lord appeared to him in a dream and set his mind at ease.

All that happened to fulfill the word of the Lord that was pronounced by the prophet: "Therefore the Lord himself will give you a sign. Look, the young woman is with child and shall bear a son, and shall name him Immanuel, which is translated as 'God with us.'" When Joseph woke up, he did what the angel of the Lord had advised him to do. He took his wife to his home. But he had no marital relations with her. "She bore a son, and he named him Jesus."

The account of Joseph's annunciation quotes the Isaiah 7:14 text, according to the Septuagint version, by modifying it somewhat. The "she shall name him Immanuel" becomes "*you are* to name him," which refers to Joseph and Mary, reinforcing, by the same token, Joseph's fatherhood. At the same time, Mary herself spoke of the "young virgin girl." In Greek, this means *parthenos* ("virgin"), which is different from [the Hebrew] *betulah*, which is more abstract and not necessarily age-related. "Conceived" is replaced by "will conceive," which brings out the text's eschatological significance.

Matthew's account is structured like the story of an annunciation. "She will bear a son, and you are to name him" (v. 21). "She shall conceive and bear a son, and they shall name him" (v. 23). "She had borne a son, and he named him" (v. 25). Verse 29 can be translated as follows: "Joseph, her spouse, who was just, and who did not want to reveal [his mystery], decided to break away in secret." Moreover, the angel's announcement was not so much aimed at making the virgin birth—which Joseph was already aware of—known. It was more to show him his *paternal role* in relation to Jesus: to take his wife Mary to his home and impose his name on Jesus.

Verses 10-21 should, therefore, be translated in this way: "Joseph, son of David, do not be afraid to take your wife Mary with you because what was conceived in her is surely the work of the Holy Spirit. But she will bear a son. You will name him Jesus, for he is the one who will save his people from their sins." When all is said and done, Joseph was righteous because he accepted the role that God had assigned him in the mystery of the Incarnate Word. He was righteous because he did not want to look like the father of the child to be born. He feared taking Mary with him since he saw himself being called by God to a mission that was better than the mission of the marriage that he had in mind.

MARY'S SILENCE

"How did Joseph judge Mary when he examined the matter in his conscience? Did he accept the idea of a miraculous intervention of God, or did he, at least, envision the

possibility? . . . We cannot prove that Joseph did not believe in a miracle. He saw a mysterious peace in Mary that
prevented from thinking badly about her. Thus, he could
have at least assumed that Mary's silence was connected
to a miracle."[16]

Joseph's Vocation

According to Pope St. Paul VI:

> The total sacrifice, whereby Joseph surrendered
> his whole existence to the demands of the Messi-
> ah's coming into his home, becomes understand-
> able only in the light of his interior life. It was from
> this interior life that very singular commands and
> consolations came, bringing him also the logic
> and strength that belong to simple and clear souls,
> and giving him the power of making great deci-
> sions-such as the decision to put his liberty imme-
> diately at the disposition of the divine designs, to
> make over to them also his legitimate human call-
> ing, his conjugal happiness, to accept the conditions,
> the responsibility and the burden of a family, but,
> through an incomparable virginal love, to renounce
> that natural conjugal love that is the foundation and
> nourishment of the family.[17]

Joseph's vocation was closely related to Mary's. According to Sertillanges,[18]

> Joseph and Mary's common vocation created a new
> connection between them. The two lilies, which
> had clashed up until then, turned toward the purple

flower—toward Jesse's Flower, whose glow lit them
up. They no longer belonged to each other, but to
the one whose destiny embraced them and, in some
way, consumed them. They thought that they would
be humanly united. Here they were united for a supernatural role, which would one day be limitless.
Mary would be the mother of humankind, being
the mother of a Church universal in time and space.
Joseph would be the patron of this same universal Church. This is the way their unequal but very
close relationship was in regard to Jesus.

According to the apocryphal and specific revelations that
were received by Maria de Agreda and Catherine Emmer-
ich, among others, Joseph would have been named to be
Mary's husband in the same way that Aaron was named to
fill the function of grandfather.

Joseph's Virginity

Mary had her heart set on this vow above everything else,"
according to Dom Marechaux:[19]

> She consented to marry Joseph. But she understood
> that she would remain a virgin. . . . Joseph was in
> Mary's presence. His very pure soul immediately
> understood, through a light of the Holy Spirit and a
> delightful anointing, that Mary had to continue to
> be a virgin and that virginity was inherent to and
> inseparable from her. Mary was inspired by chaste
> thoughts. She could only be loved with a virgin
> love.
>   At first, Joseph was won over by the veneration
> of holy virginity. The wedding between Mary and

Joseph ended with this agreement that they would entrust their virginity to each other. Mary's virginity would be an asset for Joseph, just as Joseph's virginity would be an asset for Mary. What Joseph especially loved about Mary was that she was a virgin. All his love for her consisted in carefully guarding her virginity.

About Myriam of Nazareth's answer to the celestial messenger, "How can this be, since I am a virgin?" Augustine provided the following commentary:

Here, recognize her resolve to keep her virginity. If she was going to have relations with a man, how could she have said, "How can this be?" . . . But she had the memory of her resolution, the awareness of her sacred vow, for she knew what she had promised God when she said, "How can this be? For I do not know man."

Knowing that children are only born after relations between spouses, and as she had resolved not to have those relations, when she said, "How can this be?" she was not doubting God's omnipotence; she was asking how she would become a mother. "How will this be done? What means will bring it about? You announce a son to me. You know the dispositions of my soul. Tell me in what manner this son will come to me."[20]

We can assume that Joseph was similarly resolved to remain a virgin. Between Mary and him, "there was a mutual tradition, but a tradition of two virginities. Mary's virginity became Joseph's asset. Joseph's virginity became Mary's asset. They had a right to each other, but in order to remain virgins. Their union was completed in this perfectly pure spiritual atmosphere. They were even more united because they were more chastely connected" (Dom Marechaux).

In this mutual chastity, Augustine saw a resolution on Mary's part to live a perpetual chastity. We do not need to talk about a "vow of virginity." A resolution in this respect can suffice to explain their deep disposition.

St. Bridget records that the Virgin Mary revealed privately to her that Joseph,

> before marrying me, had learned, through the lights of the Holy Spirit, that I had dedicated my virginity to the Lord and that I was immaculate when it came to my thoughts, words, and actions. This is why he married me. He only intended to behave toward me like a servant toward his lady, and to look at me as his queen. In this way, being instructed by the Holy Spirit, I knew ahead of time that even though I was the wife of a human being, through a secret provision of the adorable Providence my glorious virginity would remain intact.[21]

Joseph's Doubts

> Now the birth of Jesus the Messiah took place in this way. When his mother Mary had been betrothed to Joseph, but before they lived together, she was found to be with child from the Holy Spirit. Her husband Joseph being a righteous man and unwilling to expose her to public disgrace, planned to dismiss her quietly (Matt. 1:18-19).

The Law of Moses set a betrothal one year before the wedding. It had, however, the same legal power as the wedding. The wedding, among other ceremonies, resulted in the wife's being solemnly led to her husband's home (cf. Deut. 20:7). Once the betrothal was celebrated, the breakup of the relationship could only occur after having received a divorce decree.

Nonetheless, some people have talked at times about Joseph's "doubts." To start with, let us note that divine interventions occurred in a dream three times. The first time was when he discovered his wife's pregnancy. The second time was after the Magi left. The last time was during the return from Egypt. The angel appeared to him in his sleep. "Why did he not do it in reality," asks St. John Chrysostom, "as he did for Zachariah, the shepherds, and the Virgin Mary? Because this spouse's faith was strong. He did not need such an apparition."[22]

These dreams all ended with the assertion that the scriptures were being fulfilled: "All this took place to fulfill what had been spoken by the Lord through the prophet: 'Look, the virgin shall conceive and bear a son, and they shall name him Emmanuel,' which means, 'God is with us'" (Matt. 1:22-23). He stayed there up to the time that Herod died. Thus, what the Lord had said through the prophet was fulfilled: "Out of Egypt I have called my son" (Matt. 2:15). "There he made his home in a town called Nazareth, so that what had been spoken through the prophets might be fulfilled, 'He will be called a Nazorean'" (Matt. 2:23).

This being the case, the question deserves to be asked: did Joseph really doubt Mary when he noticed that she was expecting a child that was not his? Matthew 1:18-20 does not indicate that he doubted. We have to find the origin of this questioning in the apocryphal writings (see chapter 3). We read, first of all, in the *History of Joseph the Carpenter*, that Joseph's "mind was disturbed." We find it especially in the *Gospel of Pseudo-Matthew*: some young girls surrounded Joseph when Mary returned from her cousin's home, and he discovered that she was pregnant. They told him, "If you really want us to reveal our suspicions, nobody made her pregnant other than God's angel." But Joseph did not let himself believe that. He thought this was a deception, while wondering if Mary was not to blame or if this was a mystery.

In his *Dialogue with Trypho*, St. Justin thought that Joseph could have legitimately believed that Mary was a rape victim. This idea was also supported by Chrysostom:

> Being righteous, that is to say good and prudent, he wanted to secretly dismiss her. However, he did not wish to punish or slander her. Do you see this virtuous man, who was free of the most violent passions? You know what a great passion jealousy is. He was so free of this passion that he did not want to sadden the Virgin Mary at all. When it seemed that keeping her in his home was against the Law, and when dismissing her and leading her to prison meant the same thing as leading her to death, he did not do anything of the kind, but questioned the Law . . . . Do you see this man's prudence? Not only because he did not punish her and that he told nobody— not even her whom he suspected—but also because he was being self-reflective and striving to hide the reason from the Virgin Mary herself. The evangelist did not in fact say that Joseph wanted to drive her away, but that he wished to leave her quietly.[23]

Augustine shared this opinion. He wrote,

> The husband was worried, but the righteous man did not become violently angry. He was such a righteous man that he did not want to have an adulterous woman in his home. But neither did he want to punish the one who was dishonored. Scripture

says that he wanted to dismiss her quietly because not only did he not want to punish her. He did not even want to dishonor her offense. Pay attention to the sincerity of his fairness. For it was not to have her that he wanted to forgive her. . . . Nonetheless, he did not want to punish her. That is why we can conclude that he mercifully spared her. So, what kind of righteous man was he?[24]

And again: "Being unfamiliar with this idea, he concluded that she was adulterous." The doubt, however, was only about the decision to be made.

St. Ephrem thought instead that Mary talked it over with Joseph and that he "understood that it was a miracle of God."[25]

A second stream of thought indicates that Joseph was rather frightened to be mingled with the divine, as Jerome imagined: "He knew that she was chaste, and he was surprised by what had happened. He silently hid the mystery he did not understand."[26]

John Chrysostom thought that "the evangelist, after having shown how Mary became fertile through the working of the Holy Spirit, without any sexual relations with her husband, seemed to fear that he, a disciple of Jesus Christ, would be suspected of surrounding his Master's birth with imaginary grandeur. He thus showed us that Joseph, her spouse, was severely tested and testified to the truth of the facts. This is why he added, 'So, Joseph, her husband, being righteous.'"[27]

There is yet a third explanation of the situation, that was ventured by Hugh of Saint-Cher: Joseph was torn between his noticing Mary's pregnancy and her holiness that he could not doubt.

In the *Mystery of the Passion*[28] by Arnoul Gréban, Joseph first considered that he was deceived. Then, he could not question his wife's worthiness, which led him to summarize the situation in this way:

> God, how horrible! And do I believe it?
> No, I am lying. I still do not know. . . .
> In sum, I do not know what to think.

Gréban indicated that Joseph refused to conclude that he was betrayed without any scruples or humility on his part, which is in opposition to the traditional exegesis.

It is better to talk about "worries" rather than "doubts" or, in the end, "disturbance." This has to do with Joseph's very understandable bewilderment when he became aware that Mary, his wife, was expecting a child who was not his. However, we have seen that a number of ancient and modern authors have not admitted that Joseph could have doubted his wife's faithfulness. Convinced that he was facing a mystery, he decided on a simple secret dismissal.

The Census in Bethlehem

> In those days, a decree went out from Emperor Augustus that all the world should be registered. . . . All went to their own towns to be registered. Joseph also went from the town of Nazareth in Galilee to Judea, to the city of David called Bethlehem, because he was descended from the house and family of David. He went to be registered with Mary, to whom he was betrothed and was expecting a child (Luke 2:1-5).

According to tradition, Mary was also from the Davidic line. Tertullian interpreted the Tree of Jesse's depiction by writing that "the branch that came out of the root was Mary, who descended from David. The flower that grew from the stem was Mary's son."[29]

Joseph believed that the census "was not an act of submission to a foreign authority but a means of making his rights and credentials as a son of David known. It is precisely in the agitated periods that the official documents have a great testimonial value" (B. Martelet).

Mary and Joseph traveled the long road leading from Nazareth to Bethlehem via Samaria and the holy city of Jerusalem. When they arrived in the census town, Mary and Joseph could very logically hope to be welcomed by one of their more or less distant family members. There were many of them in the city, especially if we think about the sense of traditional Eastern hospitality.

But several factors contributed to rejecting them: the crowds who came to be listed on the registers, Mary's pregnancy, a pending birth that could complicate the lives of the hosts and force them to welcome the couple for a long time, and the appeal of a higher profit from people wealthier than from this young couple who certainly came across well, but hardly appeared to be rich.

The Savior's Nativity

"While they were there, the time came for her to deliver her child. And she gave birth to her firstborn son and wrapped him in bands of cloth, and laid him in a manger, because there was no place for them in the inn" (Luke 2:6-7).

Joseph and Mary faced the impossibility of being lodged in the city's hotel. A large inn hardly allowed for the intimacy that they wanted. The only solution that they found was to take refuge in a cave—probably a stable. The king of the world was born in this very poor place that was devoid of the amenities of a palace.

Jesus' birth occurred very discretely, and without any pomp. The Savior of the world's cradle was merely a manger of animals. It was the only decoration of the Nativity's cave. On the basis of the interpretation of Isaiah 1:3 that was offered by Origen—"The ox knows its owner, and the donkey its master's crib"—as of the fourth century, a donkey and an ox were put in the manger. They kept the newborn company.

The simplicity of the evangelical account of the birth of our Savior contrasts sharply with the extraordinary side of the apocryphal stories (see chapter 3).

The Holy Family was formed after Jesus' birth. Spiritual writers still called it the "earth's Trinity," a "created Trinity" (Jacquinot), or an "earthly Trinity," referring to the Holy Trinity or the "heavenly Trinity" with which Jesus Christ, who is both perfect God and perfect man, is connected.

JOSEPH, MARY, JESUS OR JESUS, MARY, JOSEPH?

The Holy Family's prioritized external order is the following: Joseph, Mary, and then Jesus. But its prioritized internal order, that is to say, in the realm of holiness, is the opposite: Jesus, Mary, and Joseph. Joseph visibly appeared in two extraordinary circumstances. The first one was when the elderly Simeon took the Child in his arms in the Temple on the day of the circumcision. He neglected Joseph and spoke to Mary to predict Jesus' future as well as Mary's. Then, when Jesus was found in the Temple, Joseph did not speak to Jesus. Mary did, even if she said to him, "Look, your father and I have been searching for you in great anxiety" (Luke 2:49). Thus, she put Joseph, the legal father, in the front row by putting herself in second place.

In this same circumstance, Jesus also inverted the external order: Joseph, Mary—the Child Jesus, and indicated the final prioritized order by answering: "Why were you searching for me? Did you not know that I must be in my Father's house?" He, the Son of the Father, was above Joseph and Mary, as soon as his Heavenly Father directly ordered him to do something" (Franz Michel Willam).

Jesus' Brothers and Sisters

The first point to examine on this subject comes from the writing of the Gospel according to St. Luke. Having written that Mary "gave birth to her firstborn son" (Luke 2:7), some people have concluded that she had other children with Joseph. We will come back to the virginity of Mary and Joseph in chapter 5. Here, let us say that once in Egypt a gravestone was found belonging to a certain Arsinoe, who had died giving birth to her "firstborn"—which excludes every possibility of having other children after that! Thus, the expression *firstborn* means only that this actually concerns the first child born to a woman, without requiring that there followed other children.

And logically enough, Jesus could not have entrusted Mary to John the Beloved Disciple (John 19:27) if she had had other children. That would have gone against the legal provisions.

St. Gertrude of Helfta (1256-1302) said that when she heard these words in the Divine Office "the Virgin Mary's firstborn" one day, she said to herself, "The title of *only son* seemed to be better suited to Jesus than the title of *firstborn*." The holy Virgin Mary then appeared to her and said, "No, it is not the only son, it is the firstborn son that is most suitable. For, after Jesus, my very gentle son, or, more truly, in him and by him, I have conceived all of you in the depths of my love, and you have become my sons—Jesus' brothers."

Mary was speaking here about her spiritual motherhood to all men, which was inscribed in the physical motherhood of Jesus, humanity's Redeemer.

THE HOLY KINSHIP

The *Holy Kinship* is the depiction of the family of the Virgin Mary and Jesus. At the beginning, it is limited to St. Anne, the Virgin Mary, and the child Jesus. But, starting with the apocrypha, according to which St. Anne was married three times, the depiction expanded to twenty-four people: Matthan, the father of Hismeria (who married Penter, who gave birth to Elizabeth, who married Zachariah, and was the mother of John the Baptist), and Anne. Anne's first marriage was to Joachim (who conceived Mary, the mother of Jesus), her second marriage was to Cleopas (their daughter, Mary of Cleopas, married Alpheus with whom she had James the Less, Joseph the Just, Simon, and Jude). Finally, her third marriage produced Salome, who married Zebedee and gave birth to James the Great and John the Evangelist). Starting with the fifteenth century, Anne's parents were introduced: St. Stolon and St. Emerence, her sister Hismeria, St. Elizabeth, the Holy Virgin Mary's cousin, her son St. John the Baptist, and a distant cousin named Servande.

A second question is raised because Jesus' brothers and sisters are often mentioned in the Gospels:

"While he was still speaking to the crowds, his mother and his brothers were standing outside, wanting to speak to him. Someone told him, 'Look, your mother and your brothers are standing outside, wanting to speak to you'" (Matt. 12:46-47).

"Jesus came to his hometown and began to teach

the people in their synagogue, so that they were astounded and said, 'Where did this man get this wisdom and these deeds of power? Is not this the carpenter's son? Is not his mother called Mary? And are not his brothers James and Joseph and Simon and Judas? And are not all his sisters with us? Where then did this man get all this?'" (Matt. 13:54-56).

What does this mean?

Hebrew and Aramaic do not have distinct terms to designate the different degrees of kinship. This is why the mention of Jesus' brothers and sisters in the Gospels, in reality, refers to his *cousins*,[1] who are part of the "holy kinship." For example, James and Joseph are cited in Mark 6:3 as Jesus' brothers, whereas according to Mark 15:40 they are Mary of Cleopas's sons. The phrase *Jesus' brothers* refers to the sons of another Mary, a disciple of Christ (*cf.* Matt. 27:56). She is significantly referred to as "the other Mary" (Matt. 28:1). These were Jesus' close relatives, according to an expression that is sometimes used in the Old Testament.

We find other uses of this expression. For example, in Genesis 14:14, Lot is called Abraham's brother, whereas according to Genesis 12:5 he is his nephew. Genesis 29:15 calls Laban Jacob's brother. According to Genesis 29:10, he is his uncle.

By this, we see that the mention of "the Lord's brothers and sisters" is not opposed to Mary's perpetual virginity. Moreover, we can infer from certain evangelical passages that "his brothers" were older than Jesus (cf. Matthew 12:46-50, Mark 3:31, Luke 8:19-21, John 7:3-4). This is obviously incompatible with the fact that Jesus was the Virgin Mary's "firstborn."

---

1 Or other relatives.

The Adoration of the Shepherds

In that region there were shepherds living in the fields, keeping watch over their flock by night. Then an angel of the Lord stood before them, and the glory of the Lord shown around them, and they were terrified. But the angel said to them, "Do not be afraid; for see—I am bringing good news of great joy for all the people: to you is born this day in the city of David a Savior, who is the Messiah, the Lord. This will be a sign for you: you will find a child wrapped in bands of cloth and lying in a manger."

And suddenly there was with the angel a multitude of the heavenly host, praising God and saying, "Glory to God in the highest heaven, and on earth peace among those he favors!" When the angels had left them and gone into heaven, the shepherds said to one another, "Let us go now to Bethlehem and see this thing that has taken place, which the Lord has made known to us." So they went with haste and found Mary and Joseph, and the child lying in the manger.

When they saw this, they made known what had been told them about this child; and all who heard it were amazed at what the shepherds told them. But Mary treasured all these words and pondered them in her heart. The shepherds returned, glorifying and praising God for all they had heard and seen, as it had been told them (Luke 2:8-20).

This scene is called the "adoration of the shepherds." It is striking to note that the Messiah's birth, which was long-awaited, was revealed only to people of modest means and not to the great people of this world—not even to the chief priests and the doctors of the Law. Later, under the Holy Spirit's influence, Jesus would proclaim, "I thank you, Father, Lord of heaven and earth, because you have hidden these things from the wise and the intelligent and have revealed them to infants" (Luke 10:21).

These shepherds, to whom an angel had made the good news known, came to present the earth's first accolades to its Savior. "Mary and Joseph told them more than what the Gospel says. For, when they left the cave, they not only blessed God and celebrated his praises. But they told anybody what they had seen and heard, and everyone was in awe" (Ferdinand Prat[30]).

Mary "treasured all these words and pondered them in her heart" (Luke 2:19).

Joseph's Fatherhood

Mary "will bear a son, and you are to name him Jesus, for he will save his people from their sins" (Matt. 1:21). Giving the name was the father's prerogative (cf. Luke 1:62).

We are starting with the Gospels' infancy narratives, in which the authors provide definitive details on the Incarnation of Jesus Christ, the Son of God, who came to earth to redeem all men from their sins. They were aware that they were not claiming that this was a scientific work, that is to say, they were not drawing up a genealogy with the rigor and accuracy that we would provide today.

Matthew recorded Jesus' genealogy just as St. Luke did. Their wording was not identical because the objective that the sacred authors pursued differed. The genealogy that Matthew set out starts with Abraham and goes down to Joseph, the husband of Mary, from whom Jesus was born, whereas Luke's genealogy starts with Jesus and goes back up to God the Father.

The "genealogy of Jesus the Messiah, the son of David, the son of Abraham" that Matthew offered (1:2-17) ends in this way: "Matthan the father of Jacob, and Jacob the father of Joseph the husband of Mary, of whom Jesus was born, who is called the Messiah. So, all the generations from Abraham to David are fourteen generations; and from David to the deportation to Babylon, fourteen generations; and from the deportation to Babylon to the Messiah, fourteen generations."

Luke's genealogy (3:23-38) follows the reverse order because it is aimed at the Judeo-Christian community. The author's objective is not so much to indicate a true descendance as to connect Christ to all of humanity. He gets to seventy-seven generations, reduced by the Fathers to seventy-two, which corresponds to the Table of Nations of all people (Gen. 10).

Here is that connection: "Jesus was about thirty years old when he began his work. He was the son (as was thought) of Joseph, the son of Heli . . . the son of Seth, the son of Adam, and the Son of God."

This kind of presentation is found elsewhere in the Bible for a person or family concerning the descendants of Israel's twelve tribes (1 Chron. 2:2-3, 4, and 4:1-23; 7:6-12 and 8:1-40). Jules the African (d ~240), who was succeeded by Eusebius of Caesarea (265-339), saw there an application of the Levirate law, which was presented in Deuteronomy 25:5-10. Jacob married Heli's widow. His brother died without leaving any descendants to give him a posterity. Thus, Joseph was the son of Jacob according to nature and the son of Heli according to the Law.

Matthew's genealogy is scriptural. It starts with "Abraham was the father of Isaac, and Isaac the father of Jacob . . . Jacob the father of Joseph the husband of Mary, of whom Jesus was born, who is called the Messiah" (Matt. 1:1-16). This implicitly confirms Mary's perpetual virginity, with a reference to Isaiah's prophecy (7:14) about Emmanuel, the son of the *'almah*, the "young girl." We would logically expect to read, "Joseph was the father of Jesus." So, it is very clear that Jesus was born of Mary, whereas the father was used as a point of departure for the genealogy.

The evangelist's intention was clearly to exclude Joseph's intervention in Jesus' conception while maintaining his legal fatherhood and revealing the fulfillment of the prophecy according to which the Messiah was to be from the house of David. This promise was renewed upon the return of the Babylonian exile in the person of Zerubbabel: "On that day, says the Lord of hosts, I will take you, O Zerubbabel my servant, son of Shealtiel, says the Lord, and make you like a signet ring; for I have chosen you, says the Lord of hosts" (Hag. 2:23).

The reference in this genealogy to four foreign women who became popular heroines (Tamar, Rahab, Ruth, and Bathsheba) could mean that the Messiah will announce salvation to unbelievers and prepare for the Virgin Mary's miraculous intervention. In the same way, the Magi's visit highlighted the universal nature of the "king of the Jews" who was just born: "You, O Bethlehem of Ephrathah, who are one of the little clans of Judah, from you shall come forth for me one who is to rule in Israel" (Mic. 5:2).

Matthew put the spotlight on Joseph, heir to the rights of King David, which he passed on to Jesus and to the head of the Holy Family. Jesus is the long-awaited Messiah in whom the prophecies were fulfilled. He is the son of David par excellence (1:1). His conception was virginal as foretold (1:18-24). He was born in Bethlehem when Herod was king as announced (2:1). He knew about the exile in Egypt, which was followed by Herod's massacre of the Holy Innocents (2:17-18). This was foreshadowed by the exodus that brought the people of Israel back to Egypt (Exod. 4:22) and by Rachel's inconsolable weeping when her children were deported (Jer. 31:15). Matthew then narrated the return to the region with the Holy Family's move to Nazareth (2:13-15), a despised town (John 1:46). This is a fact that coincides with the humiliated Messiah that was featured by the prophets.

Luke puts Mary, who was pondering in her heart all the events that she witnessed, in the center of his account (2:19-51). He barely mentions Joseph (1:27 and 2:48). He relates the announcement to Mary about Jesus' birth (1:26-38), the virginity appearing as a united decision between the two spouses (1:34), the visitation to her cousin Elizabeth (1:39-56), John the Baptist's birth (1:57-80), the census in Bethlehem and Jesus' nativity (2:1-14), the adoration of the shepherds (2:15-20), Jesus' circumcision in the temple, where he heard the prophecies of Simeon and Anna (2:21), Jesus' presentation in the temple (2:22-38), the return to Nazareth (2:39-40), and the finding of the twelve-year-old Jesus in the temple, where he stayed for three days without his parents' knowledge (2:41-50). We will return to these various episodes in Jesus Christ's life, all of which the holy patriarch was involved in.

We see clearly that Joseph was the protagonist of Matthew's account, whereas Mary took center stage in Luke. Luke contrasted the priest Zachariah's lack of faith (1:18-20) with the faith and humility of Mary, betrothed to Joseph (1:34-38). The story is centered on the virgin birth and the child's title of *Son of God* (1:32). This genealogy, which is between Jesus' baptism and the temptation in the desert, implies that Jesus was the New Adam. "Matthew listed the generations by going down. Luke did it by going up. Both of them did it through Joseph. Why? Because he was decisively more chaste."[31]

Mary considered Joseph to be Jesus' father (Luke 2:48). Luke the Evangelist spoke about "Jesus' parents" (2:27, 41-43). Yet Jesus' virginal conception in Mary made it impossible for Joseph to be the biological father. This clearly comes out of the Gospels (e.g., Matt. 1:18-25 and Luke 1:26-38). In his genealogy about Jesus, Luke is careful to explain that Jesus "was about thirty years old when he began his work. He was the son (as was thought) of Joseph" (3:23), implying that this was not really true.

Yet, we must recognize that Joseph's fatherhood was real and not imaginary. It was based on his marriage to Mary. When the angel instructed him to give "the name of Jesus (Matt. 1:21) to the son that Mary was going to bear, he confirmed his mission and the parental rights that, moreover, Jesus constantly respected (*cf.* Luke 2:51). When Nazareth's residents saw him confidently preaching in their synagogue, they wondered: "Is not this Joseph's son?" (Luke 4:22). Phillip presented him in this way to Nathaniel: "We have found him about whom Moses in the law and also the prophets wrote, Jesus son of Joseph from Nazareth" (John 1:45). The Jews complained about him when he introduced himself to them as "the bread that came down from heaven," saying "Is not this Jesus, the son of Joseph, whose father and mother we know? How can he now say, 'I have come down from heaven'?" (John 6:41-42).

For numerous Fathers, Jesus was conceived "without virile seed" and is "without father on earth as he is without mother in heaven." Origen asserted that "Joseph had no part in Jesus' birth, except through his service and affection. Because of this faithful service, Scripture gives him the name of father."[32] St. John Chrysostom said that the angel invited Joseph to assume the role of a father when he instructed him to give Jesus his name. And according to St. John Damascus:

> To fulfill this mission, God gave St. Joseph the love, the attention, and the authority of a father to Jesus. He gave him a father's affection so that he would very tenderly look after Jesus. He gave him a father's

attention so that he would surround him with all possible care. In the end, he gave him a father's authority so that he would be assured of being obeyed in everything affecting the Savior.[33]

Joseph's fatherhood proceeded from a direct gift of the Holy Spirit, as a heavenly fruit of his marriage. According to Dom Démaret,[34] the name that

absolutely removes every doubt, including the possibility of a false interpretation, and confirms St. Joseph's fatherhood, at the same time that it characterizes its supernatural and divine mode . . .] can claim Pius X's authority. This is because on October 11, 1906, he was pleased to grant 100 days of indulgence to be earned twice a day by all those who would recite the following prayer to the holy patriarch: "Oh Joseph, Jesus' virgin father, most pure spouse of the Virgin Mary, pray to Jesus for us every day to equip us with the weapons of grace, so that fighting according to the rule in this life, we would be crowned by him when we die."

Augustine thought that "not only did Joseph have to be a father, but he had to absolutely."[35] Hugh Ripelin of Strasbourg (1205-1270) explained that Jesus had a divine nature according to which he possessed a father, but not a mother. He had a human nature according to which he had a mother, but not a father. He possessed a spiritual nature for which he had a father and a mother.[36]

St. Francis de Sales exclaimed, "I cannot find anything that is sweeter for my imagination than to see this heavenly little Jesus between the arms of this great saint, calling him *Papa* a thousand times in his childish language with a heart in complete filial love."[37] And John Chrysostom said:

Even though Christ was conceived by the Holy Spirit, do not, however, believe yourself to be dispensed from assisting this economy of salvation. For if it is true that you did not take part in his birth and that Mary continued to be completely virgin, I, nevertheless, give you, in regard to this child, the attribute of a father in all that would not wound your virginity. I leave you with the power to give a name to your son. You are, in fact, the one who will give it to him. For even if you did not conceive him, you will be his father. This is why I unite you intimately to the one who will be born, beginning by giving him his name.[38]

The Jews, who were astonished, said this about Jesus: "How does this man have such learning, when he has never been taught?" (John 7:15). From the age of five, his father had ensured that he got a religious and moral education.

FATHER IN WHAT SENSE?

Adoptive father. This title is a misinterpretation, for a creature cannot adopt the Creator. Adoption consists in welcoming a stranger into one's family; yet Jesus was fully part of the Holy Family, whose head was Joseph. No legal act was needed to establish his fatherhood. Jesus was his son from the moment of his birth. This expression must be rejected, for "we only adopt a stranger, and Jesus was never a stranger for Joseph since he was the Son of his legitimate wife, and this wife could only have become a mother through Joseph's assent to the mystery that God favored her with. Joseph never had to adopt Jesus. He never had to complete an act of adoption for him" (L. Cristiani).[39] Fr. Sertillanges said that in reality, "Joseph did not adopt Jesus. Jesus adopted him, just as Mary did not choose the Redeemer to be her Son. The Redeemer chose her as his mother."

Legal father. This term is undoubtedly correct, but too juridical. A husband's biological fatherhood, adoptive fatherhood, or guardianship is also "legal." The first result of legal fatherhood is that the child is legitimized and receives a name and some goods. Because of Joseph's fatherhood, Jesus was given the honor of legitimacy and given the messianic title of "son of David." The Evangelist emphasized that the angel's greeting was addressed to "Joseph, son of David" (Matt. 1:20). Joseph's fatherhood was, therefore, not only legal, but truly messianic.

Foster father. Joseph was not limited to taking care of Jesus and feeding him. He had a father's heart for him. He loved him much more than any other father could have loved his children. This title, which was very present among the Church Fathers, is equivocal. It can imply that Joseph confined himself to providing for the Child's support and care; whereas the authors meant to emphasize "the faithful and constant implementation of all the functions that belong to a real father, such as caretaking, the Child's protection and education, paternal authority, the passing on of ancestral rights and even the father's deep and generous love" (R. Gauthier). Furthermore, in the strictest sense a foster father is the husband of the woman with whom a child has been fostered, who is, consequently, another woman's child.

Putative father. This is a purely negative title that was given to St. Joseph, starting with Luke 3:23. It is limited to excluding the relationship of a biological fatherhood. It is used to show that the Lord's human family was a screen destined to hide the mystery of the Incarnation from the eyes of the devil and society.

The Circumcision and Presentation in the Temple

"After eight days had passed, it was time to circumcise the child; and he was called Jesus, the name given by the angel before he was conceived in the womb" (Luke 2:21).

This rite had been instituted as a sign of the covenant that was made by God with his people: "You shall circumcise the flesh of your foreskins, and it shall be a sign of the covenant between me and you" (Gen. 17:11). This was the sign of belonging to the chosen people. But circumcision was no longer needed after the redemption that Christ brought about: "For in Christ Jesus neither circumcision nor uncircumcision counts for anything; the only thing that counts is faith working through love" (Gal. 5:6).

Although he was the Son of God as a man, "born under the law, in order to redeem those who were under the law" (Gal. 4:4-5), Jesus had to be redeemed in accordance with the prescription in the book of Numbers (18:15-16). Mary, though undefiled, had to be purified according to the prescriptions in Leviticus (12:1-8). The tradition among the Jews was that the father performed the ceremony. Joseph had to perform the rite in Mary's presence, while holding the child in his arms. The father then imposed the name on his son. According to Isidore of Isolanis, "The name of Jesus was imposed on the Savior by God, the angel, Mary, and Joseph. It was imposed by God, who gave Jesus the very thing that his name meant. It was imposed by the angel, who announced it. It was imposed by Joseph, who carried out this order."[41]

When the time had come for the purification, "they brought him up to Jerusalem to present him to the Lord (as it is written in the law of the Lord, 'Every firstborn male shall be designated as holy to the Lord'), and they offered a sacrifice according to what is stated in the law of the Lord, 'a pair of turtledoves or two young pigeons'" (Luke 2:22-24). This ceremony took place forty days after a boy's birth. The Holy Family went to Jerusalem according to the Law's prescriptions, like any other observant Jews.

> Now there was a man in Jerusalem whose name was Simeon; this man was righteous and devout, looking forward to the consolation of Israel, and the Holy Spirit rested on him. It had been revealed to him by the Holy Spirit that he would not see death before he had seen the Lord's Messiah. Guided by the Spirit, Simeon came into the temple; and when the parents brought in the child Jesus, to do for him what was customary under the law, Simeon took him in his arms and praised God (Luke 2:25-28).

Joseph was introduced as Jesus' father. Under the Holy Spirit's inspiration, the elderly Simeon recognized that the child was the Messiah and Savior. He then started singing a hymn of thanksgiving, often called the *Nunc dimittis*, starting with these words: "Master, now you are dismissing your servant in peace, according to your word; for my eyes have seen your salvation, which you have prepared in the presence of all peoples, a light for revelation to the Gentiles and for glory to your people Israel" (Luke 2:29-32).

The narrator emphasizes that "the child's father and mother were amazed at what was being said about him" (v. 33). And after that, Simeon predicted that Mary's heart would be "pierced by a sword" (Luke 2:35). He announced future sufferings, especially her son's death on the cross.

At that moment, a woman appeared. She was a prophet named "Anna the daughter of Phanuel, of the tribe of Asher." She was "a widow seven years after her marriage" and was "eighty-four." She "never left the temple but worshiped there with fasting and prayer night and day." "At that moment she came and began to praise God and to speak about the child to all who were looking for the redemption of Jerusalem" (Luke 2:36–38).

After the prescribed rites were carried out, Joseph returned with Mary and Jesus "to Galilee, to their own town of Nazareth" (v. 39).

St. Bonaventure believed that Joseph and Mary here represent the priests who offer Christ through the sacrament of the Eucharist; they who must be at once "pure, fruitful, and gentle." These virtues were symbolized by the presents offered in the temple: the turtledove, the dove, and the lamb.

CIRCUMCISION AND PRESENTATION OF JEWISH CHILDREN

The circumcision of every Jewish baby boy occurred eight days after his birth. A specialist did it in the home. The father then gave the child his name and laid his hands on him.

The presentation of Jesus in the temple was a public rite of the consecration of the firstborn to God. The child was "redeemed" by the offering of an animal. This was not mandatory. But every boy could be presented in the temple forty days after his birth and offered to God. The mother's purification had to occur beforehand—forty days after the birth. Every woman who had given birth was ritually "impure." She had to offer a sacrifice of purification that indicated her return to public life.

The Adoration of the Magi

In the time of King Herod, after Jesus was born in
Bethlehem of Judea, wise men from the East came
to Jerusalem, asking, "Where is the child who has
been born king of the Jews? For we observed his star
at its rising, and have come to pay him homage."
When King Herod heard this, he was frightened,
and all Jerusalem with him; and calling together
the chief priests and scribes of the people, he in-
quired of them where the Messiah was to be born.
They told him, "In Bethlehem of Judea; for so it has
been written by the prophet: 'And you, Bethlehem,
in the land of Judah, are by no means least among
the rulers of Judah; for from you shall come a ruler
who is to shepherd my people Israel.'" Then Herod
secretly called for the wise men and learned from
them the exact time when the star had appeared.
Then he sent them to Bethlehem, saying 'Go and
search diligently for the child; and when you have
found him, bring me word so that I may also go and
pay him homage (Matt. 2:1-8).

The accuracy of the location of the Messiah's birth in Bethlehem is taken from the book of the prophet Micah: 5:1. These
Magi, who were probably Persian scholars, dedicated themselves to astronomy. They discovered a new star in which
they saw the birth of the king of Israel proclaimed. He was
the Messiah who was eagerly awaited by the Jewish people.
They came to adore him, guided by this star, which disappeared from their view when they arrived in the holy city.

When they had heard the king, they set out; and
there, ahead of them, went the star that they had seen

at its rising, until it stopped over the place where the child was. When they saw that the star had stopped, they were overwhelmed with joy. On entering the house, they saw the child with Mary his mother; and they knelt down and paid him homage. Then, opening their treasure chests, they offered him gifts of gold, frankincense, and myrrh (Matt. 2:1-11).

ST. JOSEPH'S SILENCE

"He is silent like the earth at the time of the dew" (P. Claudel).[42]

Pope Pius XI declared that between

> two great people [John the Baptist and the apostle Paul], the person and mission of St. Joseph appeared. They, nevertheless, went by in silence and were unnoticed and misunderstood, in humility and silence. It was a silence that would only be illuminated centuries later. But the deeper the mystery, and the thicker the night that covered it, and the deeper the silence, the higher the mission was. The procession of virtues that was required and the merit that, happily, had to respond to such a mission were richer. This unique grandiose mission, which included taking care of the Son of God—the king of the Universe—protecting Mary's virginity and holiness, and cooperating as the only one called to participate in the great mystery—hidden from the centuries—of the divine Incarnation and the Salvation of the human race" (March 19, 1928).

He never talked. He thought, listened, and obeyed. There was something in him that was

> powerful and calm, which made you think about the universal and peaceful attention of the heavenly Father ruling over the world" (R. Guardini).[43]

The Magi are considered to be the first fruits of the Gentiles who were called to receive Christ's salvation. (The popular tradition made them kings for no real reason.) There were three of them: a symbol of the Holy Trinity, taking into account the number of gifts that Matthew mentioned. "On entering the house, they saw the child with Mary his mother; and they knelt down and paid him homage. Then, opening their treasure chests, they offered him gifts of gold, frankincense, and myrrh" (Matt. 2:11).

Tradition has also given us their names: Melchior, Gaspar, and Balthazar. They are celebrated on Epiphany day, from the Greek *epiphaneia*—"apparition." This is the day when Jesus Christ's divinity was openly manifested. It is also the first time that non-Jews recognized Jesus' divinity. From then on, it was considered to be the first announcement of truth to the Gentiles.

"And having been warned in a dream not to return to Herod, they left for their own country by another road" (Matt. 2:12). Evidently, this upset the sinister plans that Herod slyly organized. St. Jerome noted that "this response was not given to them by an angel, but by the Lord himself to show the privileged character of Joseph's virtues."[44]

The Flight to Egypt

"Now after they had left, an angel of the Lord appeared to Joseph in a dream and said, 'Get up take the child and his mother, and flee to Egypt, and remain there until I tell you;

for Herod is about to search for the child, to destroy him.'
Then Joseph got up, took the child and his mother by night,
and went to Egypt" (Matt. 2:13-14).

Egypt evokes the patriarchs' travels: Abraham went there
(Gen. 12:10) as well as Jacob, who settled there (Gen. 46:2-
5). But this country is, above all, the land where the chosen people had been reduced to slavery; from where God,
through Moses' intervention, brought them out to settle
them in the Promised Land.

The angel (Matt. 2:19-21) ordered Joseph the patriarch
to go to Egypt, just as Moses had been ordered to return to
Egypt after staying in Midian (Exod. 4:19-20). The texts are
strikingly similar:

> The Lord said to Moses in Midian, "Go back to
> Egypt; for all those who were seeking your life are
> dead." So Moses took his wife and his sons, put
> them on a donkey, and went back to the land of
> Egypt" (Exod. 4:19-20).
>
> An angel of the Lord suddenly appeared in a
> dream to Joseph in Egypt and said, "Get up, take the
> child and his mother, and go to the land of Israel, for
> those who were seeking the child's life are dead."
> Then Joseph got up, took the child and his mother,
> and went to the land of Israel (Matt. 2:19–21).

According to Jerome, the evangelist "did not say, 'He
took his son and his wife,' but 'the son and his mother,' as a
foster father and not as a husband."[45]

Jesus was the new Moses and the new Israel. Herod
played the same role as Pharaoh. Jesus relived the history of
his people: Pharaoh's persecution and the liberation of the
Exodus, which is the archetype of all liberations, including
the one that followed the Babylonian exile. But Archelaus,

Herod's son, reigned in Judea. Also, Joseph went down to the "Galilee of the Gentiles" (Matt. 4:15; Isa. 8:23), that is to say, in a Gentile region.

F.M. Willam muses:

> The angel had ordered them to head toward Egypt. A flight toward the north was not possible. A flight toward the east, where the desert followed the desert, was also impossible for Mary in the current circumstances. The shortest path to leave the territory that was subject to Herod's domination was the one that led to Egypt. But this path consisted of several hundred kilometers.
>
> A question arises. Did Mary and Joseph know that God had ordered the Magi in a dream not to return to Herod? The Magi must have had this dream in Bethlehem; otherwise, they would have started their trip by heading toward Jerusalem. But, if they'd had the dream in Bethlehem, they would have certainly informed Mary and Joseph about it, assuming that they had the time to do it. It is even possible that God had warned the Magi and St. Joseph during the same night. . . .
>
> From Bethlehem, which was situated at an altitude of about 800 meters above sea level, one had to go down to the lowland. From there, strictly speaking there was no path, but rocky trails that only animal hoofs and men's feet maintained, from century to century. They went on this trip partly taking advantage of the night.
>
> At dawn, from the top, they noticed the Philistine region at their feet. They lay down in the plain under the atmosphere's blue vapors. . . .
>
> On the second day, they reached Gaza, which

was the last rather important city before the desert. They bought some things in preparation for the desert voyage.

Then, the immense solitude began.

Joseph and Mary probably did not cross the desert by themselves. As they had to travel across a territory that had no water and stick to a set schedule, in order to reach campsites that had been planned, Easterners organized themselves and traveled in groups.

According to some traditions, the Holy Family traveled not only in Egypt but also in Ethiopia. First, it stopped in Oun, or Heliopolis, which was twelve miles from Babylon in Lower Egypt, where Cairo stands today. A Jewish colony lived in this city for many years. Having, little by little, grown and become rich, it possessed a temple and a Bible—that is to say, the temple of Leontopolis, a neighbor of Heliopolis, and Greek copies of Scripture, which were used by Jews in Alexandria.

JOSEPH'S LOVE FOR JESUS

God, having chosen this great saint to be Jesus' Father, must certainly have put a fatherly love of such a lovable son, who was God, in his heart. Joseph's love was, therefore, not only natural, like the love of other fathers, but even supernatural because he found his son and his God in the same person. Joseph knew, through the angel's certain and divine revelation, that this Child, who always accompanied him, was the divine Word who, for the love of men, and him in particular, became man. He knew that this adorable Chad chosen him among everyone to be the guardian of his life and wanted to be called his son. Imagine what a fire of love all these considerations must have lit in Joseph's heart when he saw his divine Master serve him as a simple laborer who opened or closed the store, helped saw the wood, handled the plane or the ax, picked up the chips, and swept the house. In a word, he obeyed him in all that he ordered him to do and did nothing without depending on his authority.[40]

Nonetheless, the holy spouses did not stay there for very long. According to the common tradition, they went into a little village called Mataria, which was a mile from Heliopolis and around 500 kilometers from Bethlehem. (A Franciscan who went on this same trip in the seventeenth century wrote, "You have to consent to stay twenty-three days on top of a camel and be exposed to the evening dew as well the excessive heat of the sand, which is lit by the sun's heat. During the one hundred leagues that the trip lasts, you do not come across a stone or spring.") Having rented a humble dwelling there, they lived as poor and unknown people. Joseph practiced his trade as best he could. Mary helped him to support his family through her work.

Joseph remained in Egypt until "the death of Herod. This was to fulfill what had been spoken by the Lord through the prophet, 'Out of Egypt I have called my son'" (Matt. 2:15). We find this prophecy in Numbers 24:17.

How long did the stay in Egypt last? We have to guess. In the past, it was estimated that the exile lasted seven years. But [modern] exegetes "think that when the children in Bethlehem were massacred, Herod was in the last years, if not the last months of his life. According to this estimate, the stay in Egypt may have only lasted a few months, and must not have gone on for more than two or three years" (B. Martelet).

The Holy Family had barely arrived at the borders in Gaza, and even Ascalon, when Joseph heard some sad news. When Herod died, a great deal of turmoil had exploded in Jerusalem. Archelaus, since the first days of his reign, had shown himself to be his father's worthy son by killing 3,000 Jews, most of whom had taken refuge in the temple.

> When Herod died, an angel of the Lord suddenly appeared in a dream to Joseph in Egypt and said, "Get up, take the child and his mother, and go to the land of Israel, for those who were seeking the child's life are dead." Then Joseph got up, took the child and his mother, and went to the land of Israel. But when he heard that Archelaus was ruling over Judea in place of his father Herod, he was afraid to go there. And after being warned in a dream, he went away to the district of Galilee. There he made his home in a town called Nazareth, so that what been spoken through the prophets might be fulfilled, "He will be called a Nazorean" (Matt. 2:19-23).

Joseph feared this region's unrest, for it seems that his first thought had been to go to Bethlehem, which was not far from Jerusalem, and to settle there permanently. He thought that it was appropriate to settle where Providence had the Messiah be born. He took the Ascalon path in order to avoid Judea completely. From there, he went to Joppe and then to Caesarea Maritima. Next, slanting to the right, he went through the rich countryside of the Esdrelon plain and sank into the Galilean mountains. This province was then subject to Antipas, Herod's second son, who was less cruel than the others. The small city of Nazareth is in these mountains.

The Massacre of the Holy Innocents

Meanwhile, a tragic episode took place.

When Herod saw that he had been tricked by the wise men, he was infuriated, and he sent and killed all the children in and around Bethlehem who were two years old or under, according to the time that he had learned from the wise men. Then was fulfilled what had been spoken through the prophet Jeremiah [31:15]: "A voice was heard in Ramah, wailing and loud lamentation, Rachel weeping for her children; she refused to be consoled, because they are no more" (Matt. 2:16-18).

THE NUMBER OF VICTIMS

How many victims were there? Nobody knows. Bethlehem had to have around 2,000 residents. Because there was so much infant mortality, everything leads us to believe that there were no more than thirty boys who were two years old and younger in Bethlehem and its surroundings. Even for this limited number, the massacre of the children in Bethlehem, which was ordered by Herod, was a horrible crime. The Church celebrates these innocent and unknowing little victims as real witnesses to Christ" (B. Martelet).

Ordinary Life in Nazareth

The return to Nazareth was not free from difficulties of adjustment. Joseph and Mary could expect to be extensively questioned about their reasons for not returning after the census and for their prolonged absence.

For us, the people of Nazareth's questions shed an even brighter light on the importance of the trip to

Bethlehem and the flight to Egypt in the general plan of Jesus' life. Their absence from Nazareth had widened the gap that separated Mary and Joseph from their spousal kinships. In this way, the mystery that they alone had been taught remained hidden. It was revealed only to the shepherds, the Magi, Simeon, and Anna in the temple. These were people heaven had chosen in accordance with the law of grace and not according to the law of kinship. . . . Thus, it is true to say that Jesus grew up "in obscurity" in Nazareth even though Joseph and Mary were known to everyone as far back as the time that preceded his miraculous birth" (F.M. William).

When they arrived in Nazareth, the Holy Family began to have an ordinary life, which is often considered to be a "hidden life," for nothing drew attention to it. It took place just like any other life: consisting of work, family life, friendship, leisure, and prayer.

THE CARPENTER

St. Joseph appears as a practicing carpenter in the Gospels. "Is not this the carpenter, the son of Mary?" (Mark 6:3), the residents in Nazareth wondered when Jesus came to preach in their synagogue. This text could have included, in a primitive version that was confirmed by Origen and Papyrus 45 in the third century, "the son of the carpenter," as we read in St. Matthew's parallel passage (13:55): "Is not this the carpenter's son? Is not his mother called Mary? And are not his brothers James and Joseph and Simon and Judas?"

Even regardless of the apocrypha's testimony, the social status of a carpenter was supported by tradition. In the third century, St. Justin wrote that Jesus made "plows and

yokes for oxen." The Syrian, Coptic, and Ethiopian versions
went in the same direction. The word *carpenter*, which is
translated from the Greek *tekton*, refers to the *faber lig-
narius*, the woodworker, and can be understood in a broad
sense to mean carpenter, wheelwright, builder, mason. (See
chapter 5 for more.)

By his closeness with Jesus and Mary, Joseph sanctified
ordinary life and work in the Holy Family's home. In the atmosphere of truth, simplicity, and intimacy, which reigned
in its midst, nothing distracted Joseph and Mary in their
single and common concern—Jesus and the fulfillment of
his divine mission. St. Bernard drew a lesson from this. Just
as the shepherds did not find the child to be alone, but with
Mary and Joseph, "Mary, Joseph, and the child in the manger must always be in us," that is to say—the child's humility, the virgin's purity, and Joseph's justness. "This righteous
man had such a beautiful place in the gospel."[46]

Bossuet believed that "Joseph was honored to be with
Jesus Christ every day and that he, along with Mary, had no
greater share in his graces. Nevertheless, Joseph was hidden,
and his life, actions, and virtues were unknown." He adds,

> Perhaps we can learn from such a good example
> that we can be great without being famous, that we
> can be blessed without noise, that we can have real
> glory without the help of being world famous, but
> only through the witness of one's conscience. . . . To
> hear the greatness and dignity of Joseph's hidden life
> solidly, let us go back to the principle. Let us, above
> all, admire the infinite variety of God's guidance in
> different vocations.

Curiously, the same Bossuet thought that ordinary life in Nazareth was more extraordinary than the Passion that was experienced by our Lord in Golgotha, "for, in the end, I would not be afraid to say, o my Savior: I know you better on the cross and in the shame of your torment than I do in this lowliness and unknown life."

In Nazareth, Jesus himself learned from Joseph, who exercised his paternity toward him:

> Jesus' obedience to his mother and legal father fulfilled the fourth commandment perfectly and was the temporal image of his filial obedience to his Father in heaven. Jesus' everyday obedience to Joseph and Mary both announced and anticipated the obedience of Holy Thursday: "Not my will. . . ." (Luke 22:42). The obedience of Christ in the daily routine of his hidden life was already inaugurating his work of restoring what the disobedience of Adam had destroyed" (cf. Rom. 5:19)" (*Catechism of the Catholic Church* (CCC) 532).

This submission of the Son of God is surprising in itself. Is he not the Master of the universe? St. Bernard wondered,

> Who then was submitted, and to whom? A God was subject to men. This is a God, I say, whom the angels, principalities, and powers obey. He was subject to Mary, and not only to Mary, but also to Joseph, because of Mary. Let us admire both of them and, choose what you prefer, be it the Son's exquisite condescension or the mother's very eminent dignity. Either way, it is an amazing miracle."[47]

Pope St. John Paul II reflected:

What is crucially important here is the sanctification of daily life, a sanctification that each person must acquire according to his or her own state, and one that can be promoted according to a model accessible to all people: "St. Joseph is the model of those humble ones that Christianity raises up to great destinies . . . he is the proof that in order to be a good and genuine follower of Christ, there is no need of great things–it is enough to have the common, simple and human virtues, but they need to be true and authentic" (Paul VI) (*Redemptoris Custos* 24).

THE RIGHTEOUS MAN

If the Holy Spirit called Joseph a rigteous man when he was chosen to be Mary's spouse, let us consider all of the divine love and virtues our saint must have collected from the conversations and continual companionship of his holy spouse in whom he saw a perfect model of all the virtues. If only one of Mary's words was enough to sanctify John the Baptist and fill Elizabeth with the Holy Spirit, we must think that Joseph's beautiful soul must have become really holy through his intimate relationship with Mary, in the space of at least twenty-five years, according to tradition! (St. Alphonsus Liguori).[48]

Calling St. Joseph a *righteous man* amounts to confirming that he possessed, not only the virtue of justice, but also all the supernatural virtues, in the sense of the Scripture passage: "The righteous flourish like the palm tree" (Ps. 92:12), and "his righteousness endures forever" (Ps. 112:9). This is St. John Chrysostom's doctrine: "He calls a man who is gifted with all the virtues *righteous*—justice being all virtues. It is especially in this sense that Scripture uses the word *justice* when it expresses itself in this way: righteous and true man."[49]

Paul Claudel reflected that "Joseph is the patron of the hidden life. Scripture does not mention any of his words. Silence is the Word's father. He was so full of contrasts! He is the patron saint of celibates, family men, laypeople, contemplatives, priests, and businessmen."[51]

Canisius provided the testimony of Eusebius of Emesa, according to which Mary, who did not have any brothers, was the only one to collect her parents' estate. He also quoted Nicephorus Callistus Xanthopulus, who thought that Mary and Joseph not only had a home in Nazareth but owned property as well. According to Fr. Mora, "After his marriage, the immaculate spouse's paternal home became his. Nonetheless, he did not stop spending time in his workshop."

We could say that Matthew was essentially interested in four questions:

1. "*Who* is Jesus?" The genealogy (1:1–17) then answers this question. His identity, which is illustrated by his ancestors, is confirmed through his divine and Abrahamic lineage.

2. The second scene (1:18–25) answers the question of "the *how*" of Jesus' identity. He is the son of David, not because he was conceived by one of David's descendants, but because Joseph, who was from the Davidic line, accepted him as his child.

3. The following account (2:1–12) answers the question of *where* Jesus was born. He was born in Bethlehem, which emphasizes his identity as a son of David. The Magi, who were Gentiles, reacted to this birth in faith, thus manifesting that Jesus was really Abraham's son (1:1).

4. Finally, three short accounts—the flight into Egypt, the massacre of the children in Bethlehem, and the settling in Nazareth (2:13–23)—set Jesus' destiny in motion and respond to the question, "*Where* did Jesus come from?" Jesus providentially used the experiences of Moses in Egypt and Israel during the Exodus. He was moved from Bethlehem, the city of the king of the Jews, into Egypt, and to the Galilee of the Gentiles. He was going to live in Nazareth. Hence, according to Matthew, he was called a Nazarene (Gérard Rochais[52]).

JOSEPH, JESUS' GUARDIAN

How does Joseph exercise his role as protector? Discretely, humbly, and silently, but with an unfailing presence and utter fidelity, even when he finds it hard to understand. From the time of his betrothal to Mary until the finding of the twelve-year-old Jesus in the temple of Jerusalem, he is there at every moment with loving care. As the spouse of Mary, he is at her side in good times and bad, on the journey to Bethlehem for the census and in the anxious and joyful hours when she gave birth; amid the drama of the flight into Egypt and during their frantic search for their child in the temple; and later in the day-to-day life in the home of Nazareth, in the workshop where he taught his trade to Jesus. How does Joseph respond to be the protector of Mary, Jesus and the Church? By being constantly attentive to God, open to the signs of God's presence and receptive to God's plans, and not simply to his own . . .

Joseph is a "protector" because he is able to hear God's voice and be guided by his will; and for this very reason, he is all the more sensitive to the persons entrusted to his safekeeping. He can look at things realistically, he is in touch with his surroundings, he can make truly wise decisions. In him, dear friends, we learn how to respond to God's call, readily and willingly, but we also see the core of the Christian vocation, which is Christ! Let us protect Christ in our lives, so that we can protect others, so that we can protect creation!"[53]

In reality, St. Joseph appears to us not only as Jesus' conscientious guardian, "but, with Mary, he personifies the most selfless aspect of parents' friendship toward their child. Just as someone's love goes into the person who is being loved, St. Joseph, to use Ubertino of Casale's expression, was entirely transformed in Jesus, who was the object of his daily contemplation. This was done to such an extent that we could . . . summarize Joseph's activity toward Jesus in a few words: "A far-sighted and arduous love to meet all the divine child's needs. A strong and courageous love to shield him from the wrath of his enemies. A tender and affectionate love to be inseparably attached to him" (Billuart) (R. Gauthier).

St. Joseph's Mission

Joseph was predestined, from all eternity, to the dignity of being Mary's spouse and Jesus' foster father. Predestination is the eternal design of God's will through which he predicted that some men—God's elect—would be eternally happy.

Predestination includes not only the coming glory, but also all the graces that are granted throughout one's life to do this effectively.

The Congregation for Divine Worship and the Discipline of the Sacraments wrote that

in his providential wisdom, God carried out his plan of salvation by assigning a particularly important mission to Joseph of Nazareth, a "righteous man" (Matt. 1:19) and the Virgin Mary's husband (Luke 1:27). On the one hand, this entailed legally introducing Jesus into the Davidic line, from which, according to the Scripture's promise (2 Sam. 7:5-16; 1 Chron. 17:11-14), the Messiah and Savior was to be born. On the other hand, he was going to take on the job of being this child's father and guardian.

In accordance with this mission, St. Joseph was very much present in the mysteries of the Savior's childhood. He received the revelation of the divine origin of Mary's motherhood from God (Matt. 1:20-21). He was the privileged witness of Jesus' birth in Bethlehem (Luke 2:6-7), of the adoration of the shepherds (Luke 2:15-16), and the adoration of the Magi who came from the East (Matt. 2:11). He carried out his religious task in regard to the child by bringing him into Abraham's Covenant during his circumcision (Luke 2:21) and giving him the name of Jesus (Matt. 1:21).

According to the Law, he presented Jesus at the temple, and redeemed him by offering the gift to the poor (Luke 2:22-24; Exod. 13:2.12-13). He was very amazed while listening to Simeon's prophetic canticle (Luke 2:25-33). He protected the mother and son during Herod's persecution by fleeing to Egypt (Matt. 2:13-23). Every year, he went to Jerusalem with Mary and the child for the Passover feast and fearfully witnessed the event of the disappearance of the twelve-year-old Jesus, who stayed in the temple (Luke 2:43-50). He lived in the family home in Nazareth while exercising his paternal authority over Jesus, who was obedient to him (Luke 2:51). He taught Jesus the Law and his carpenter's trade (*Directory on Popular Piety and the Liturgy* 218).

Joseph's mission, first of all, regarded Mary's virginity, which he was called to preserve while in a true marriage with her. Then, it was about the child Jesus, whose father he was, according to the proper preface of St. Joseph. In the third place, it had to do with the mystery of the Incarnation, which was to be revealed to Joseph in order for him to be able to protect his spouse's virginity and ensure the Son of God's education. Joseph experienced the expectation of the Messiah's coming:

> The messianic hope distinguished the Jewish religious soul. The religion's passion was turned toward the future. It was a marvelous future when the Messiah would bring his people salvation and establish a kingdom whose master would be God. Joseph was deeply filled with this hope and waited for this new era more impatiently than others. . . . He recalled the prophetic oracles [Jer. 31:33, Ez. 36:25-29] that had announced a new covenant in which the people would really belong to their God, with a new spirit and heart" (J. Galot).

According to the Church Fathers, Joseph was the type of the apostles who brought Christ to the Gentiles (Hilary of Poitiers) and the face of Church pastors, especially the bishop (Ambrose). They went so far as to establish an analogy between the earthly craftsman, Jesus' father in the view of men, and the heavenly Craftsman—the Word's Father.

> From this twofold dignity flowed the obligation which nature lays upon the head of families, so that Joseph became the guardian, the administrator, and the legal defender of the divine house whose chief he was. And during the whole course of his life he fulfilled those charges and those duties. He set

himself to protect with a mighty love and a daily solicitude his spouse and the Divine Infant; regularly by his work he earned what was necessary for the one and the other for nourishment and clothing; he guarded from death the child threatened by a monarch's jealousy, and found for him a refuge; in the miseries of the journey and in the bitternesses of exile he was ever the companion, the assistance, and the upholder of the virgin and of Jesus (Leo XIII, *Quamquam Pluries*).

The Finding of Jesus in the Temple

St. Luke explained that when they returned from the presentation of Jesus in the temple, "the child grew and became strong, filled with wisdom; and the favor of God was upon him" (2:40).

However, the happy period of contemplation of their son was darkened by an event that filled the hearts of Mary and Joseph with anguish. The Law required the Jews to go to the temple in Jerusalem three times a year, especially on the occasion of the Passover feast, in order to offer their adoration and sacrifices to the Lord God. The trip that St. Luke talked about (2:41-52) is probably not the first one that the divine Savior participated in, for "every year his parents went to Jerusalem for the festival of the Passover" (Luke 2:41). When he was twelve years old, the age when Jewish boys made their *bar mitzvah*, "they went up as usual for the festival" (Luke 2:42).

The Law did not order presence in Jerusalem for longer than the eight days of the Passover feast. But the pilgrims who came from far away surely rested for a while. "Mary and Joseph undoubtedly spent the whole week in Jerusalem. The last day of the feast was celebrated like a Sabbath. It was

a kind of 'day after the holiday'—something like the Feast
of St. Stephen, Easter Monday, or Pentecost Monday today.
The 100,000 pilgrims could not naturally set out on their
journey at the same time" (F.M. Willam). People traveled in
caravans by leaving around noon. On the first day, the trip's
stage was a short one. The location of the first stopover was
agreed upon when they departed.

"When they were returning from there at the end of the
week, the boy Jesus stayed behind in Jerusalem, but his parents did not know it. Assuming that he was in the group of
travelers, they went a day's journey. Then they started to
look for him among their relatives and friends" (Luke 2:43-
44). That the child Jesus, who was already twelve years old,
was found to be by himself on the occasion of a pilgrimage
is completely plausible because children could travel either
with their father or mother. The men and women traveled
in separate caravans. But at the end of the day, while the pilgrims were grouped into families, Mary and Joseph had to
admit that Jesus was absent, despite their searching.

Mary and Joseph probably turned back that very evening, or else had to wait for the light of the next day, which
would have made the time even more painful. They questioned all those they met. "When they did not find him,
they returned to Jerusalem to search for him" (Luke 2:45).
The main source of their anxiety probably came from their
knowledge of the scriptures that foreshadowed a suffering
and tormented Messiah.

> Had the Passion already started? The thought that
> Jesus could already suffer what the prophets had
> heralded and that he would suffer without them tore
> their hearts out. Or, as some prophets had been, was
> Jesus mysteriously taken away by the Spirit without
> anyone's knowing where he had left him or when
> he would reappear? (B. Martelet).

"After three days they found him in the temple, sitting among the teachers, listening to them and asking them questions. And all who heard him were amazed at his understanding and his answers" (Luke 2:46-47). It is likely that Jesus participated in teaching children his age and, as his parents noted, in talking with the temple teachers.

"When his parents saw him they were astonished; and his mother said to him, 'Child, why have you treated us like this? Look, your father and I have been searching for you in great anxiety.' He said to them, 'Why were you searching for me? Did you not know that I must be in my Father's house?'" (Luke 2:48-49). They do not seem to have thought about it.

MARY AND JOSEPH, THE COUPLE

Mary is reported to have said to St. Bridget of Sweden:

Joseph served me as his sovereign. As for me, I stooped to provide him with the smallest services. Joseph and I did not keep any riches for ourselves— only what we needed to give us the necessary strength for God's service. We sacrificed what we did not need and gave it to the poor for the love of God. On the other hand, we were always satisfied with the little that we had.

I had been destined from all eternity to sit on a magnificent throne and be honored above all men. However, in my humility, I did not deign to serve Joseph and to prepare everything that was necessary for us. When he served me, Joseph never let any words that were casual, muttered, or angry fall from his lips. He was very patient in his poverty and very active in his work, when he had to be. He was also

> very gentle with those who spoke harshly to him,
> very considerate in the services that he provided
> me, and very careful to defend me against those
> who attacked my virginity. He was the very faithful
> witness of divine wonders.
>
> He was so dead to the world and the flesh that
> he wanted only heavenly things. He had such faith
> in God's promises that he often cried out: *May I
> love long enough to see God's will be fulfilled!* He
> spent little time with men and their gatherings. His
> only desire was to obey God's laws. His glory is now
> great.[50]

Mary and Joseph, who witnessed this scene, shared in the doctors' astonishment, not because they were unaware of where the child got such wisdom, but because it was the *first time that he manifested it in public*. "In the midst of the joy of the sudden encounter," Fr. d'Alès[54] writes, "Mary could not forget what she had suffered. She did this without any bitterness. But she admitted this to her son with loving abandon and asked him to explain why. This 'why' was the counterpart of the 'how' that was spoken to the angel on the day of the Annunciation. There was no disbelief there. There was no criticism here."

Jesus responds to the virgin's *why* with another *why*. He wanted, in this circumstance, to make those his Father had entrusted to him understand that he had to keep being completely independent in his mission. Refraining from all criticism, he alluded to the mystery of his divine lineage.

Jesus did not correct his parents "because they searched for him as their son," explains the Venerable Bede. "But he enlarged their vision so that they would see all that they owed the one whose eternal Son he was." He had to be with his Father—that is to say, in the temple, a "house of prayer" (Luke 19:46), as he would later say. According to another translation, Jesus responded to his parents that he had to be about his Father's business and thus, first and foremost, take care of what his mission was—the reason for his coming to earth. He would say, one day while resting from the weariness of the road, while seated on the edge of Jacob's Well: "My food is to do the will of him who sent me and to complete his work" (John 4:34). He demonstrated, by these words, that he intended that he would always and in everything only do what was pleasing to his Father (cf. John 8:29).

For St. Bonaventure, Joseph and Mary here represented the doctors and preachers who were looking for Jesus in the scriptures. One of St. Anthony of Padua's sermons points to Joseph as the symbol of poverty, to Mary as the symbol of humility, to Simeon as the symbol of penance, and to Anne as the symbol of obedience.

Luke added that Mary and Joseph "did not understand what he said to them" (2:50). The Holy Family then went back on the road to Nazareth where Jesus would live in obedience to his parents. His mother "treasured all these things in her heart" (Luke 2:51).

Joseph's Death

Scripture does not say anything about when Joseph was called back to God. It seems that he died before our Lord's Passion, because otherwise Jesus would have had to entrust Mary to him and not to John the apostle. We can consider a practical reason for this: if Joseph had lived when Jesus had started to preach, it could have hindered his mission because people would have thought that Jesus was talking about him when he mentioned his Father.

Some people believed that when Jesus started his public life, he no longer needed Joseph because he had carried out his mission as the "Redeemer's guardian." Others thought Joseph died soon after the finding of Jesus in the Temple, after which, Joseph is no longer mentioned. "The common view is that he died when he was around sixty years old and before the time that our Lord left Nazareth to receive John the Baptist's baptism" (Patrigniani[55]).

We know that St. Joseph's death was honored. It was a death "of love," like Mary's, according to St. Francis de Sales. In the Greek Catholic liturgy, the eighth ode of the March 19 matins reads:

Happy Joseph, your death was fulfilled in God's hands. In fact, you were purified since your childhood, and you became the guardian of the one who had been filled with every blessing. You and she cried out while saying, "Bless the Lord, all you works of the Lord; sing praise to him and highly exalt him forever" [Dan. 3:57]. The righteous Joseph truly embraced the Creator God before whom all immaterial creatures tremble, and he embraced him as a child. He received a spiritual light from him, and he gloried in it.

"The presence of such a spouse and child," writes St. Alphonsus Liguori, "made Joseph's death very sweet and precious. How, in fact, could the death of the one who died in the arms of life have ever been bitter? Who could ever express or understand the pure delights and consolations, the blessed hopes, the acts of acceptance, and the flames of love that gave Joseph's heart words of eternal life that Jesus and Mary alternately spoke to him during these last moments?" Joseph's death, continues Liguori, was completely peaceful and smooth. It was free of anxiety and fear because his life had always been pure. . . . Happy the soul who, in these final struggles, will be protected by this great saint! For, having died between the arms of Jesus and Mary, and having freed the child Jesus from the danger of death by transporting him into Egypt, he was privileged to be the patron of a happy death and free his dying servants from the danger of eternal death.[56]

Without a doubt, writes Father Patrignani,

In that moment, Jesus would have paid for all of Joseph's moments of fatigue through floods of inner joy, all his tears by so many heavenly consolations, and all his anguish by guaranteed pledges of confidence and peace. He supported his languishing head with one hand. With the other one, he pressed this same heart where He so often rested when He was a child. He lovingly squeezed it. Mary thanked her husband for his holy companionship and the affectionate care that he had given her.

Mary's words were, for the dying man, so many arrows of love that consumed him. This caused some people to say that it was love alone that made St. Joseph die. Be that as it may, the Church sometimes compares his death to a peaceful sleep . . . and sometimes to an aromatic burning torch that dies by radiating the smooth odor that entered into its substance. We can envy the death of the saints because they all died in God's kiss. But this kiss is not real. It is merely a sweet and precious feeling of love. Joseph truly died in God's kiss.[57]

According to Gerson,[58] Jesus himself washed Joseph's body, crossed his hands over his chest, which he then blessed to preserve him from the corruption of the tomb. He ordered the angel to keep an eye on him until the time when he was placed in his fathers' tomb, between Mount Zion and the Mount of Olives. In the apocryphal *History of Joseph the Carpenter* (see chapter 3), Joseph died when he was 111 and Jesus was eighteen. In this account, on his deathbed, Joseph bitterly regretted his lack of understanding of the miracle of the Incarnation.

The *History of Joseph the Carpenter* places Joseph's tomb in Nazareth, just like the Alexandrian synaxarion. The Greek liturgy maintains that he died on July 20, as does the Syro-Jacobite liturgy, and the Ethiopian liturgy asserts that it was on August 2. In the sixteenth century, the Sacred Congregation of Rites twice rejected the perception that the date of the holy patriarch's death was to be set on July 20. Yet, this was still supported by Cardinal Lépicier, who also argued that Joseph's death occurred after the second year of our Lord's public life:

> We read in St. Matthew that when Jesus arrived in Nazareth, he was poorly welcomed by his fellow citizens, who expressed themselves in this way: "Is not this the carpenter's son? Is not his mother called Mary? And are not his brothers James and Joseph and Simon and Judas? Where then did this man get all this?"
>
> In considering these expressions, we will notice, first of all, that all the people that are named here, either specifically, or generally, were supposedly still alive when the Nazarenes were speaking in this way. But, above all, what was said about the carpenter was particularly meaningful. In Greek, it is

referred to by the article, which gives us the following meaning: "Is this Jesus not the carpenter's son, whom we all know?"

In order to understand the full force of this reasoning, we must recall that when our Lord was living, as well as now, there was only one carpenter whom everyone recognized as such in small towns like Nazareth. He was a kind of official carpenter. When he died, another carpenter took his place. Thus, if, during the time that we are talking about, St. Joseph had already died, Jesus could not have merely been called a carpenter's son. Joseph's name would have to have been added to indicate what carpenter it was. Even more so, to avoid all confusion, this name should have been added if there had been several other carpenters in Nazareth then and if Joseph had died. Let us recall that this happened after the second Passover of Jesus' public life, that is to say, before he sent his apostles off to preach the kingdom of God for the first time.[59]

JOSEPH'S ASCENSION

Pope St. John XXIII wrote that "we can devoutly believe that the deceased people in the Old Testament who were closest to Christ—let us mention two who most intimately participated in his life—John the Baptist the Precursor and Joseph of Nazareth, his foster father and guardian—are honored and privileged to open up this admirable support on the way to heaven. They are also honored to burst into the first notes of the endless *Te Deum* of the human generations that have departed in the footsteps of Jesus the Redeemer toward the glory and grace that are promised to the faithful."

Joseph's Resurrection

This was a pious belief that was created from Matthew 27:52-53. After Christ's death on the cross, "the tombs were opened, and many bodies of the saints who had fallen asleep were raised. After his resurrection they came out of the tombs and entered the holy city and appeared to many."

St. Bernardino of Siena wrote in this respect that

> if God the Savior had wanted to glorify Mary's body as well as her soul on the day of her Assumption, in order to satisfy his devotion to his parents, we can and must devoutly believe that he did not do any less for Joseph. He was so great among all the saints that Jesus gloriously raised him from the dead on the day when, after having risen from the dead himself, he pulled others out of the tomb's dust.[60]

Cardinal Lépicier was inspired by the transporting of Joseph the patriarch's bones by the Hebrews who were going to Canaan. He thought that "such a devout feeling could not have failed to arouse the divine Savior to bring the bone structure of the most holy and pure husband of his mother out of the sepulcher in order to get him into heaven with him soon, where he would be calm, immortal, subtle, and beaming with glory."

St. John XXIII declared that it was plausible that the bodies of St. John the Baptist and St. Joseph were assumed into heaven (Feast of the Assumption, 1960).

Heaven and St. Joseph

Our Lord assured us that, in the afterlife, his Father "will render to each according to his actions" (Matt. 16:27). Alphonsus Liguori commented:

> What glory he must have bestowed on St. Joseph, who loved him so much and had offered so many services during his life on earth. On the last day, the Savior will say to his elect: I was hungry and you gave me food, I was thirsty and you gave me something to drink, I was a stranger and you welcomed me, I was naked and you gave me clothing.
>
> However, others have only fed, lodged, and clothed him in the poor, whereas St. Joseph provided food, a home, and clothing to Jesus himself. Moreover, the Lord promised a reward to whomever gives even a cup of cold water to one of these little ones in his name (Matt. 10:42). Thus, how great Joseph's reward would be. He could say to Jesus Christ, "I not only provided you with food, a home, and clothing, but I saved your life by delivering you from Herod's hands!"[61]

We can also say that, since the mystery of the Incarnation towers over everything, the glory of Joseph in heaven is superior to that of the other saints, with the exception of the Virgin Mary. God promised that the one who welcomes "a righteous person in the name of a righteous person will receive the reward of the righteous" (Matt. 10:41). It seems to go without saying that he had to give Joseph a reward that was worthy of the splendor of the God whose earthly father and guardian he was, and that the angel would specifically describe Joseph as a "righteous man" (Matt. 1:19).

This presence in heaven was the source of an incomparable joy for Joseph. St. Bernard wrote that

> we must not doubt that Jesus Christ, when he was alive on this earth, showed signs of intimacy and respect, as a son should toward his father, and that in heaven, he would not deny offering them to him. On the contrary, he would expand on and perpetrate them. This is why Jesus said, "Enter into the joy of your master." He did this in order to make us understand, in a mystical way, that not only is this joy in him. It also surrounds and absorbs him on every side, drowning him as if he were in an endless chasm."[62]

ST. JOSEPH'S GLORY

St. Bernadino of Siena asserted, before the residents of Padua: "Could we believe that the arms that held the Savior for so long would remain buried in the dust of the deceased? How can we think that Jesus Christ did not admit this sacred body, which was his earthly shield, into his heavenly palace? Yes, St. Joseph is glorious in heaven. He reigns there in body and soul." Olivi believed that "it was impossible to doubt the intimacy and respect that Christ showed him on the earth, like a son toward his father. He did not refuse them in heaven but perfected them instead."

St. Francis de Sales and many others after him maintained that St. Joseph is in glory, both in body and soul. Joseph comes immediately after Mary in the celestial hierarchy. This makes him an advocate *par excellence* for men, according to Charles of St. Paul. This author stressed that our saint is wearing the three crowns that are suitable for martyrs, confessors, and virgins.[63]

Dom de Marechaux explained the reasons for this:

> The gospel teaches us that our Lord wanted companions of his glorious Resurrection. St. Matthew told us that when Jesus died, "the tombs also were opened, and many bodies of the saints who had fallen asleep were raised. After his resurrection they came out of the tombs and entered the holy city and appeared to many" (Matt. 27:52-53). How could it be that Jesus, having chosen an escort of the resurrected in order to assure his own Resurrection and to make his victory shine more, would not include Joseph, his adoptive father, among them, and put him in the front row? Joseph had all the titles for this honor. They were titles that were similar to those that earned Mary her glorious Assumption, namely, his quality as Mary's husband, Jesus' adoptive father, and the head of the Holy Family.

St. Joseph exceeded all the saints and angels in glory. In fact,

> The Lord, from all eternity, predestined St. Joseph to the dignity of being Mary's husband and Jesus' putative father, a dignity that he thought placed him above all creatures right away and let him fulfill his mission as perfectly as possible. He lifted him up in grace from one degree to another until he had reached all the merits in the divine decrees. This gave him the right to the celestial crown that he was destined for. St. Joseph perfectly accomplished all that God had decreed in this organization of ideas in the order in which it was implemented. In this

way, the unique spot that he occupies in heaven is
both God's free gift and the fruit of his own merits
(Cardinal Lépicier).

Joseph and the Passion

Cardinal Lépicier again explained why God did not want
Joseph to witness the Passion:

The aim of the mission that was entrusted to St.
Joseph was to cover the mystery of the Incarnation
like a veil to put a stop to the indiscreet and mock-
ing looks of an unbelieving generation. The noble
and very important service of nourishing the divine child, defending and protecting his life, and,
in a word, preserving it, in preparation for the great
sacrifice, was attached to this mission. But, when
the time that God set up drew near, when the Savior willingly headed toward death, the death on the
cross, Joseph's mission had to stop. The holy patriarch was to disappear to allow the mother of Jesus,
who was linked to the sacrifice, to be by herself. She
offered the Lord's divine victim to humankind.

This service of immediately cooperating with Jesus in the work of our redemption must belong ex-
clusively to this admirable woman, who had given
him our nature. When this solemn tragedy was to
take place, St. Joseph needed to move away from the
theater of the redemption to let the light shine on
the two great reasons for our salvation. These were
reasons that were perfectly subordinate: Christ and
his mother.

Nonetheless,

> St. Joseph participated, more than anyone, after the most holy Virgin Mary, in the Passion of Christ. His pains, as a whole, were greater than any creature could bear because of his inseparable union with Jesus and Mary. The sea of bitterness of these two was reflected in Joseph's heart. On the other hand, in proportion to this union, there was the greatest knowledge of this horrible mystery of pain that occurred on Holy Thursday, whether it was through the angel's revelation and Simeon's prophecy or Jesus' intimate secrets and the hints that the Holy Spirit put in his soul.
>
> Through the voluntary acceptance of his vocation as father and lord of the family that was predestined to be the instrument of the world's salvation (*causa salutis*) and his generous gift to participate in the Lord's cross, in order that it would fulfill all men more, St. Joseph's painful cooperation was the greatest one ever after Mary's. Like hers, it was unique in that he participated with the Redeemer in the objective, and not merely applicative, redemption. It was incomparably greater than the one that can be attributed to other saints (Ferrer Arrellano[64]).

PART II

St. Joseph

in the

Bible

Joseph Heralded in the Old Testament

From the Greek *typos,* meaning "type," *typology* is the interpretation of Scripture that "discerns in God's works of the Old Covenant prefigurations of what he accomplished in the fullness of time in the person of his incarnate Son" (CCC 128).

It is traditional to compare Joseph, the Old Testament patriarch, with Joseph, Mary's husband. St. Bernard makes this parallelism very clear:

> Remember now that the patriarch with this name who was sold in Egypt. Not only did he have the same name, but he also had his chastity, innocence, and grace. In fact, the Joseph who was sold by his brothers who hated him and led him into Egypt, was the face of the Christ who was also sold. Our Joseph, in order to avoid Herod's hate, took Christ to Egypt (Matt. 2:14). In order to remain faithful to his master, the first Joseph did not want to share his mistress's bed (Gen. 39:12). The second one, who recognized his lover in his Lord's mother, the Virgin Mary, faithfully observed the laws of abstinence. The one was given the understanding of dreams. The other one was allowed to be the confidant of heaven's designs and cooperate with them. One put wheat in reserve, not for himself, but for his people.

The other one received the bread of heaven, not only for his people, but also for his himself.

We cannot doubt that this Joseph, whom the Savior's mother was betrothed to, was a good and faithful man, or rather, the faithful and careful servant whom the Lord placed near Mary in order to be his mother's consoler, the foster father of his physical body and the faithful cooperator of his great work on earth. Let us add to this that he was from the house of David, according to the Evangelist. This noble Joseph showed that he, in fact, descended from this royal source—from David's very blood through his birth. But he was even more noble through his heart.[65]

Because of his marriage to Mary, the face of the Church, Joseph appeared, in turn, as Christ's model. From Christ, we go to the pope, his vicar on earth. Joseph is also a type of God the Father, the artisan of all things, or of the sanctifying Spirit. And Joseph is yet the model of the Church.

Abraham

Some people do not hesitate to compare Joseph to Abraham, just as Jesus is compared to Isaac, starting with the first chapter of the Gospel according to St. Matthew. In fact, just as Abram received the word of God in a vision, the angel appeared to Joseph in a dream. The Lord told Abram not to fear, and the angel said the same thing to Joseph. Abram complained to the Lord that he did not have children; Jesus, like Isaac, was born of a "sterile" woman, and even if was not a "sterility" like Sarah's, there was a miraculous pregnancy in both cases. The angel's announcement was identical: "She will bear you a son, and you shall name him Isaac (Gen. 17:19) and Jesus" (Matt. 1:23).

Jacob

Jacob, who was a patriarch in the Old Testament, was the son of Isaac and Rebecca, Esau's brother, and Abraham's grandson. He also received the name of Israel after his struggle with a mysterious "man" who is traditionally identified as an angel of God or the angel Gabriel (Gen. 32:24-30). Some authors (such as Origen and Ambrose) see him as a figure of Joseph. For example, after having obtained the promise of paternal heritage for his posterity, Jacob fled, on his mother's advice, to Mesopotamia, to get away from his brother's deadly hatred. As Joseph had received the promise of the kingdom of God for the divine child, he fled to Egypt, on the angel's advice, to get away from Herod's persecution.

According to Cardinal Lépicier, "Because of the charity that stimulated him, which corresponded to the gift of wisdom, Joseph was covered with a coat of glory. He received an unsurpassed power in the Church, along with the task of providing for the needs of the faithful."

We also see Jacob's prophecy confirmed in him: "I give you a share in addition to the one that belongs to you and your brothers," as if he said, explains Denis the Carthusian, that "because of your exceptional virtues, and for the blessings you have given my family and me during the famine, I entrust you, rather than your brothers, with a heritage, as a special gift . . . as a sign of the special affection that I have for you."[66]

Joseph

A patriarch of the Old Testament, one of Jacob's twelve sons, he is the first known man to bear the name of *Joseph*. Since the prayer of his mother Rachel, who had been sterile for a long time, had been answered, she called her first son Joseph, that is to say, "May the Lord add to me another son!" (Gen. 30:24).

His story was told in chapters 37 to 48 in the book of Genesis. He was sold as a slave by his brothers, who were jealous because his father favored him. He was led into Egypt and became the country's most powerful man—Pharaoh's prime minister. Having been warned in a dream of a long famine's upcoming arrival, Joseph accumulated wheat reserves. When the people cried out to Pharaoh to have some bread, he responded: "Go to Joseph (*Ite ad Ioseph* in Latin); what he says to you, do" (Gen. 41:55).

Jacob's sons came to buy wheat in Egypt. Joseph ended up being recognized by them. Then, he had them come to Egypt with their elderly father, where they settled in the land of Goshen.

The *Ite ad Ioseph* was taken up by a Christian devotion to invite us to go to St. Joseph, from whom we receive Jesus, "the living bread that came down from heaven" (John 6:51).

The interior life is none other than a constant and intimate relationship with Christ in order for us to identify ourselves with him. Joseph knows how to tell us many things about Jesus! This is why you must never neglect spending time with him: *Ite ad Joseph*, as the Christian tradition has repeated with a phrase from the Old Testament.

Joseph was a master of the interior life, a hard worker at his job, and a faithful servant of God, who was constantly connected to Christ. *Ite ad Joseph*. With St. Joseph, the Christian learns what it means to be of God and totally committed to being among men by sanctifying the world. Go to Joseph, and you will find Jesus. Go to Joseph, and you will find Mary, who always filled Nazareth's charming workshop with peace.[67]

St. Peter Chrysologus (406-450), theologian, bishop of Ravenna, adviser to Pope Leo I, and Doctor of the Church, was the first one to compare Joseph the patriarch of the Old Testament to St. Joseph. He thought that both Josephs seemed almost merged into one person (*Sermon* 146). Pope St. Leo XII added:

> Beyond the fact that the same name—a point the significance of which has never been denied—was given to each, you well know the points of likeness that exist between them; namely, that the first Joseph won the favor and especial goodwill of his master, and that through Joseph's administration his household came to prosperity and wealth; that (still more important) he presided over the kingdom with great power, and, in a time when the harvests failed, he provided for all the needs of the Egyptians with so much wisdom that the king decreed to him the title "savior of the world."
>
> Thus it is that we may prefigure the new in the old patriarch. And as the first caused the prosperity of his master's domestic interests and at the same time rendered great services to the whole kingdom, so the second, destined to be the guardian of the Christian religion, should be regarded as the protector and defender of the Church, which is truly the house of the Lord and the kingdom of God on earth. These are the reasons why men of every rank and country should fly to the trust and guard of the blessed Joseph" (*Quamquam Pluries*).

St. Bernard of Clairvaux (1090-1153) also established this parallel:

Remember that this great patriarch who came to Egypt, from whom Joseph not only inherited the name, but the chastity, innocence, and graces. The first Joseph, who was sold by his jealous brothers and brought to Egypt, clearly prefigures Christ who was sold by Judas. The second Joseph, getting away from Herod's hate, brought Christ to Egypt. The first one, by being faithful to his master, rejected the advances of this master's wife [Gen. 39:7-23]. The second one, who was also chaste, respected the virginity of his wife, the mother of his Lord. The first one received the gift of understanding dreams. The second one was privileged to know heaven's secrets and have a share in them. The one made money, not for himself, but for all the people. The living bread coming down from heaven was entrusted to the other one, who had to keep it both for himself and for the entire world. There is no doubt that this Joseph, to whom the mother of the Savior was betrothed, was a good and faithful man and a reliable servant. The Lord had him support his mother. He provided food for his body and was the only one on earth who assisted his great work.[68]

Blaise Pascal wrote that Jesus Christ was

typified by Joseph: the beloved of his father, sent by the father to see his brethren, etc., innocent, sold by his brethren for twenty pieces of silver, and thereby becoming their lord, their savior, the savior of strangers, and the savior of the world, which had not been but for their plot to destroy him, their sale and their rejection of him. In prison, Joseph innocent between two criminals; Jesus Christ on the cross between two thieves. From the same omens, Joseph foretells freedom to the one and death to the other. For the same sins, Jesus Christ saves the elect and condemns the outcast. Joseph foretells only; Jesus Christ acts. Joseph asks him who will be saved to remember him when he comes into his glory; and he whom Jesus Christ saves asks that he will remember him when he comes into his kingdom.[69]

Moses

"Moses was very humble, more so than anyone else on the face of the earth . . . my servant Moses; he is entrusted with all my house. With him I speak face to face—clearly, not in riddles" (Num. 12:3-8). These qualities of gentleness and faithfulness to keep the deposit that was entrusted to him, and the knowledge of supernatural things, were found in Joseph. He received the great grace of learning directly from the one who is "the Truth" (John 14:6).

St. Irenaeus reflected:

Wherefore also Moses giving a type, cast his rod upon the earth, in order that it, by taking life, might expose and swallow up the opposition of the Egyptians that was lifting itself up against the pre-arranged plan of God; that the Egyptians themselves might testify that it is the finger of God that works salvation for the people, and not the son of Joseph. For if he were the son of Joseph, how could he be greater than Solomon, or greater than Jonah, or greater than David, when he was generated from the same seed, and was a descendant of these men? And how was it that he also pronounced Peter blessed because he acknowledged him to be the Son of the living God"?[70]

David

We are emphasizing David's humility, and his justice high-lighted by the Holy Spirit himself—"I have found David the son of Jesse, a man after mine own heart, which shall fulfill all my will" (Acts 13:22)—as well as the glory of having the very wise King Solomon as his son. These are all qualities that can also be found in Joseph, patron of the hidden life, accomplishing what God asked of him and becoming the father of the king of the universe and the Creator of all things.

Joseph and the Lord's Poor

In the Old Testament, we gradually see how the "little remnant of Israel" remained little, poor, humble, and modest. It withstood Israel's trials, which were experienced as successive purifications. Zephaniah proclaimed, in the name of the Lord, "I will leave in the midst of you a people humble and lowly. They shall seek refuge in the name of the Lord—the remnant of Israel; they shall do no wrong and utter no lies, nor shall a deceitful tongue be found in their mouths" (Zep. 3:12-13).

The Lord's poor form a community, which is certainly not structured but whose members share the same attitude of inner humility, openness to God, and expectation of his salvation. They can belong to different social classes, but their origins are usually modest.

In the New Testament, we find an environment of the Lord's poor, as opposed to the Sadducees, Pharisees, and Zealots. "Mary, Joseph, Elizabeth, Zachariah, Anne, and Simeon belonged to this environment of the Lord's poor. They were like Israel's finest flower—the ones in whom all the expectations of their people were concentrated—the ones that the Messiah would be living in. It is said that the *Magnificat* is the ultimate song of the poor, which expresses their home" (Pierre Robert).

John the Baptist and St. Joseph

"Among those born of women no one has arisen greater than John the Baptist; yet the least in the kingdom of heaven is greater than he" (Matt. 11:11).

"The kingdom is the New Testament. St. John, 'the greatest person' in the Old Testament, stayed at the New Testament's gate. St. Joseph is, along with Mary, the first one to belong to the kingdom" (L. Cristiani). John the Baptist was not privileged to share the existence of Jesus and Mary. Joseph did not see the Savior from far away—the "Lamb of God," as John the Baptist called him to his disciples (John 1:36). Rather, he carried him in his arms and cared for him in every way.

The Apostles and St. Joseph

Joseph surpasses the apostles in the order of predestination (see chapter 1). Cardinal Lépicier explained it in this way:

> In the hierarchy of the Church Militant, the apostles, in view of their mission of establishing and ruling over the Church of Jesus Christ, received free gifts that were better than those of St. Joseph, whose mission was humbler and more hidden. Yet, the holy patriarch's mission of watching over the life of the Church's founder and of nourishing and defending him, took on a greater importance than that of ruling the Church and spreading the gospel.

Bossuet indicated the differences between Joseph's mission and that of the apostles:

Among all the vocations, I notice two in the scriptures that seem to be directly opposed. The first one is the apostles'; the second one is Joseph's. Jesus was revealed to Joseph, but in very adverse conditions. He was revealed to the apostles to be announced throughout the universe; He was announced to Joseph to keep him quiet and hide him. The apostles were lights to show Jesus to the world; Joseph was a veil to cover him. Mary's virginity and the greatness of the Savior of souls were hidden under this mysterious veil.[71]

St. Joseph and the Angels

Being predestined by God to a state of life allowed Joseph to keep growing in divine grace. Joseph not only became worthy of being chosen as the spouse of the Savior's mother—he also enjoyed, more than any other saint, an intimate exchange with the Incarnate Word, producing new acts of charity without ceasing.

Cardinal Lépicier wrote that we can conclude

that the holy patriarch was predestined to a degree of glory that assured him of the spot that was left empty by the rebellious angels, that is to say, Lucifer. This enabled him to occupy the most elevated position in the order of the Seraphim. By his example and exhortations, the first prevaricating angel led the others to revolt. On the other hand, St. Joseph was predestined to this incomparable glory to order to help men, by his example and noble patronage, called to eternal bliss. This is the reason the holy patriarch was solemnly declared the patron of the universal Church.

JOSEPH AND JOAN

A parallel has even been drawn with St. Joan of Arc, one of France's secondary patrons. Father Benoisey wrote in this respect:

> Oh! There were certainly many differences of nature, race, religion, and time between them! But there were also similarities! In fact and first of all, both of them had the same modest origin. St. Joseph undoubtedly belonged to a royal race. The Church honors him as David's illustrious descendant. But his family fell from its ancient grandeur. Joseph, a modest carpenter, was forced to earn his living by the sweat of his brow. St. Joan of Arc did not have a noble status. Being the daughter of farmers, she split her time between working in the fields, taking care of the livestock, and housework. God is pleased to lift up the humble and look for his assistants among the weak.
>
> This is why he chose St. Joseph and St. Joan of Arc. For, if both of them had very ordinary occupations, they, nonetheless, lifted them up and sanctified them by praying, by offering them to God, and by being charitable toward those who were unfortunate and disadvantaged. They were already holy, and the holiness of their existence drew God's gaze upon them. . . .
>
> There is another way in which they are alike. God tasked them with completing a mission. He sent an angel to Joseph who bore this message: "Joseph, son of David, do not be afraid to take Mary as your wife, for the one she will give birth to is the Savior the world is waiting for." God entrusted the

archangel St. Michael to Joan. "There is much pity in the kingdom of France. daughter of God, go save France." Both of them, of course, were aware of their inability. They defended themselves from undertaking the task that God was entrusting to them. Joan protested, "I am only a humble girl." But the archangel reassured her and promised that she would be protected by St. Catherine and St. Marguerite. Joseph was scared about the thought of becoming the husband of his God's mother and the master of his God. The angel simply responded, "Do not be afraid."

So, what were these missions? St. Joseph needed to ensure the child Jesus' conditions of human existence and defend from Herod the one who would be the Savior of men. Joan received the mission of saving the king of France, who was merely the poor king of Bourges. By saving him, she would be saving France, the eldest daughter of the Church, from England's heretical yoke. To accomplish this task, Joan left her country and went far away from her family to struggle, toil, and suffer. Joseph would impose the same sacrifices on himself. First, he fled Nazareth, his workshop, and his relatives to go to Bethlehem. Then, he went to Egypt with Mary and the child.

There is one more similarity between them: their admirable chastity. St. Joseph remained pure. He became Mary's husband only to guard her virginity. St. Joan of Arc heroically practiced the virtue of chastity in Domremy among her young companions and on the battlefields in the midst of immodest and rude soldiers who surrounded her and never dared to disrespect her. But how cautious she had to be in order to make sure that she was given this respect!

The destinies of St. Joseph and St. Joan of Arc were so similar when they were alive. They continued to look alike after their deaths. Oblivion very quickly covered Joseph under a thick mantle. The Gospel and Tradition no longer talked about him. People had to wait until the fifteenth century in order for them to think of him and start honoring him. . . . St. Joan of Arc's memory knew the same fate.

Claude Quinard[72] introduced this parallel:

On the day of the temple, the one with the flowering branch [that saw Joseph chosen as Mary's spouse] was, for Joseph, this circle of darkness. And in this struggle, in his faithfulness to what is good, in the suffering of all that he voluntarily shattered, and in his abnegation of life's passions, God's favor descended on him. As envisioned in this way, Joseph's figure shows up to be very high and really distant from cold imageries and timid words! The Maid of Orléans' epic poem, which is so popular, is not more moving. The voices' search for the young girl is completely related to the angel who was received in a dream.

PART III

St. Joseph

in the

Apocryphal Writings

The word *apocryphal* comes from the Greek *apo*, "far," and *krypto*, "to hide." It applies to written works whose divine inspiration the Church does not recognize. Consequently, the canonical books in the Old and New Testament are excluded. Here, we are citing those apocryphal written works where Joseph is mentioned in one form or another.[2]

The Protoevangelium of James

The oldest of the known apocryphal [Christian] writings were written in Greek around 130 to 140. It was fully preserved and shows how much interest there was in Mary then—ascribing to her a life that was dedicated to God and holy from the time she was an infant. It includes the most holy Virgin Mary's life up to the Annunciation, an account about Jesus' nativity and the adoration of the Magi, the massacre of the Holy Innocents, and Zachariah's murder. It treats Mary's virginity and her education in a way that today we could describe as "quasi-monastic." It used materials from the second century.

When she is twelve, Mary leaves the temple ("so that she would not stain the sanctuary"). She is entrusted to Joseph

2 Editor's note: though not canonically recognized as inspired, these works can give us insight into early Christian traditions about New Testament figures.

the carpenter, for a dove came out of his rod. Joseph was a widower: "I have sons, and I am an elderly man." Having taken the "Virgin Mary under his protection," Joseph leaves to construct his buildings, while Mary weaves for the temple's veil.

Chapters 14 to 16 describe Joseph's astonishment in seeing Mary pregnant. He is accused of violating his matrimonial commitments. Both of them are subjected to a trial that establishes their innocence. Joseph leaves to go work at his construction sites. Mary stays in Elizabeth's home for three months. "From day to day, her womb was getting rounder. She was worried and went back to her home. She hid from the sons of Israel. She was sixteen years old when these mysteries came about."

Her sixth month arrives, and Joseph returns from the building sites. He goes into the home and notices that she is pregnant. He strikes his face and falls to the ground on his sackcloth. He cries bitterly while saying,

> "What brow will I raise before the Lord God? What prayer will I speak to him? I welcomed her as a virgin in the Temple of the Lord, and I did not keep an eye on her. Who betrayed me? Who committed this crime under my roof? Who kidnapped the virgin and contaminated her? Did the story of Adam repeat itself on my behalf? For when Adam was saying his prayer of praise, the serpent approached him and only surprised Eve. He seduced and contaminated her. The same disgrace is striking me." Joseph rose from his sackcloth and called Mary: "You, who are God's favored one, what did you do? Did you forget the Lord your God? Why did you disgrace yourself—you who were raised in the Holy of Holies and fed from an angel's hand?"

Mary cries, saying, "I am pure and do not know any man." Joseph says to her: "Where is the fruit of your womb coming from?" She replies: "As true as the Lord my God is living, I am unaware of where he is coming from." Joseph, afraid,

> remained silent and wondered what to do with her. He told himself: "If I keep her fault secret, I will be breaking the law of the Lord. But if I denounce her to the sons of Israel, and her son comes from an angel, which I am very afraid of, I will be handing innocent blood over to a death sentence. What will I do with her? I will secretly repudiate her."
>
> The night crept up on him in his thoughts. And an angel appeared to him in a dream, saying, "Do not be afraid to take Mary as your wife, for the child conceived in her is from the Holy Spirit. She will bear a son, and you are to name him Jesus, for he will save his people from their sins." Joseph woke up and glorified the God of Israel who had given him his grace. And he kept the young girl. Annas the scribe came to see him and said, "Joseph, why did you not come to our meeting?" He responded, "My trip tired me out, and I spent the first day resting." But Annas turned around and saw that Mary was pregnant.

The second part opens with Augustus's edict, Mary's ambiguous status—Joseph wonders: how will I enroll her? As my wife or my daughter?—and Mary's vision of two people. While sometimes laughing and sometimes crying, Mary confides in Joseph while they are on the way to Bethlehem of Judea. She sees "two people before my eyes. One of them crying and mourning, the other one rejoicing and reveling."

At mid-route—the place was a desert—Mary senses that what is inside her is "pressing to get out." Joseph leads her to a cave and goes to look for a midwife. Then follows Joseph's vision and the story about the suspension of time, the silence of nature, and the stillness of all living things in announcing the Messiah's birth.

The Acts of Thomas

This apocryphal publication, which belongs to a gnostic tradition, is known for its liturgical hymns. In the "Hymn of the Liberator" (143:3), Christ is greeted as the one "who came from above, appeared through the Virgin Mary, and is called the son of Joseph, the carpenter."

The Gospel of Thomas

This apocryphal book, with numerous revisions in Greek, Latin, Georgian, Slavonic, and Armenian, goes back to a Syrian source before the year 400. Combined with the *Protoevangelium of James*, it has inspired stories of Christ's childhood ever more extravagant and fanciful—among them the *Armenian Gospel of the Infancy* and the *Arabic Infancy Gospel*. It devotes a lot of space to the Virgin Mary's life. Joseph's role in this book is important but thankless. Jesus is portrayed as a temperamental and ill-behaved boy. Here is a sample:

> Jesus was walking in the village, when a child, while he was running, bumped him on the shoulder. Jesus was irritated and told him: "You will not continue on your way." At that moment, the child collapsed and died. When they saw this, some people cried

out, "Where does this child, whose every word becomes real, come from?" The young boy's parents complained to Joseph: "With a child like yours, you must no longer stay in the village with us— or else teach him to bless rather than curse. For he makes our children die." Joseph took his son aside and scolded him: "What got into you? These people are suffering. They hate us and want to drive us away!" Jesus responded: 'I know that the words you just said are not coming from you. So, for your own sake, I will be silent. But they will receive their punishment." The complainants were immediately blinded.

The History of Joseph the Carpenter

This apocryphal text that was written with the aim of being edifying devotes a lot of space to the life of Jesus' mother while rather faithfully following the evangelical accounts. Here is how it starts:

> This is [the account] of the death of our holy father Joseph the carpenter—Christ's father according to the flesh. He lived to be 111 years old. Our Savior told his entire biography to the apostles on the Mount of Olives. The apostles themselves wrote these words and dropped them off in Jerusalem's library. The holy elderly man abandoned his body on the twenty-sixth of the month of *Abib* [between June 25 and July 24].

This work, which was probably written in the fifth century, has been fully preserved. Christ in person recounts the life and death of the holy patriarch. Jesus expands on Joseph's first marriage, which yielded four boys—Jude, Joset, James, and Simon—and two girls—Lysia and Lydia. When Joseph took Mary into his home, she "found little James being like a sad orphan there. She started to pamper him. This is why she was called Mary, the mother of James."

Jesus cannot hold back his tears at the sight of Joseph dying. "When my father Joseph said these things, I could not stay without shedding tears, and I cried when I saw that death overcame him, and when I heard the distressing words that he was saying."

"I myself, my friends," he continues, "I sat at his bedside. . . he looked up and let out a loud groan. . . . When my dear mother saw me feel his body, she also felt his feet. She found that his breathing and warmth were gone. . . . The Virgin Mary, my mother, and I cried [with Joseph's other children], for the time of death had arrived."

The Ascension of Isaiah

This was written at the end of the first century, and a part of it sets out to explain Mary's virginity and purity. "So, I saw a woman from the line of the prophet David named Mary. She was a virgin and espoused to a man named Joseph. He was a carpenter by trade and also descended from David the righteous man from Bethlehem in Judea." Upon finding Mary to be pregnant, Joseph wishes to repudiate her, but the angel of the Spirit appears to him, and he stays with her.

After two months, Joseph is in his home with Mary. They are by themselves. While they are alone, Mary looks up and notices a small child. She is astonished. She then finds herself as she was before her pregnancy. As her husband Joseph asks her why she is astonished, having opened his eyes wide he becomes aware of the child. Then, he praises God because the Lord had become his inheritance (11:2-15).

The Epistle of the Apostles

Epistola Apostolorum, which was written between 160 and 170, develops a teaching—in the form of a dialogue—that goes from Christ's preexistence through the Incarnation to the Second Coming. The book starts with a profession of faith in which the apostles testify that Jesus "is the Word who became the Virgin Mary's flesh in his sufferings and was conceived by the Holy Spirit." He was born from God's will and not from the lust of the flesh, and "was swaddled at Bethlehem," was known and educated, and grew up. "Joseph and his mother Mary" sent him to school.

The wedding feast at Cana is also mentioned. Christ is invited to attend "with his mother and brothers." Nonetheless, the miracle is performed without his mother's intervention. His mother is also absent on Easter morning. Later, Christ uses some elements of his disciples' profession of faith.

The Arabic Infancy Gospel

This was inspired by the *Protoevangelium of James*, the *Gospel of Thomas*, and the *Story of Joseph the Carpenter*.[3]

The account deals with Jesus' childhood, showing us an attentive and active Virgin Mary. She tells Joseph that the birth is about to occur and that her pain is not letting her

---

3 Editor's note: and like those gnostic texts it contains many fantastical accounts, including the claim that Jesus miraculously aided Joseph's work "for Joseph was not very skillful in carpentry"(!).

continue. She suggests that they go into the cave. She thanks the Magi and gives them one of the child's swaddling clothes as a gift. They recognize "a divine thing" in them.

The account of the Holy Family's stay in Egypt comes after that, along with miraculous healings performed by Jesus.

The Gospel of Pseudo-Matthew

Also called the "Book of the Birth of Blessed Virgin Mary and the Savior's Childhood," its author is unknown. It was also inspired by the *Protoevangelium of James* and the *Gospel of Pseudo-Thomas*.

The prologue claims that it was written by "the blessed priest Jerome" to tell the truth about some apocryphal books that are full of heresies. But, in various manuscripts, the prologue assures that the author is "James, son of Joseph." (This contradicts the beginning, but proves that the Latin text is very dependent on the *Protoevangelium of James*.) We read that Joseph had grandchildren and that the temple's authorities entrusted him not only to Mary but to "five other young girls who were to be with her in Joseph's home." These young girls witnessed Mary's chastity.

Two days after the Nativity, it is said that Mary left the cave, "went into a stable, and dropped the child off in a manger," where he found his faithful companions—the ox and the donkey. The subsequent flight into Egypt is colorful and full of extraordinary claims, in order to demonstrate the child Jesus' divinity and great humanity. After Mary complains about the heat, Joseph puts her under a palm tree. Mary regrets not being able to gather fruits, and Joseph responds that he is more preoccupied by the lack of water. Jesus then commands the palm tree to stoop to Mary's level and make water gush out of its roots.

The Latin Infancy Gospels

These apocryphal writings, dated from 500 to 800, follow the usual pattern of the canonical Gospels regarding Jesus' infancy and are heavily inspired by the *Protoevangelium of James*. They start with the presentation of Mary's parents and end with Zachariah's murder and the coming of John the prophet in the desert.

We find a very strong legendary trend in the accounts of the birth, the shepherds, and the Magi. Christ's birth, as reported by the midwife, resembles an epiphany of light.

The Gospel of the Nativity of Mary

This work, which was written at the end of the ninth century, is considered to be an excerpt from the *Gospel of Pseudo-Matthew*. It was borrowed to some extent from the *Protoevangelium of James*, while being inspired by the childhood stories of Matthew and Luke. It more fully develops the miracle of the pigeon and Joseph's rod.

Mary, by herself, without union with a man, virgin, will conceive a son; a servant, she will conceive the Lord; eminent by her name and work, she will conceive the Savior of the world. Moreover, Jesus' birth will be pure and sinless. The angel Gabriel is sent to Mary to make her know about the Lord's conception and explain the way it was going to be done. "Do not think, Mary, that you will conceive in a human manner. It is without union with a man that as a virgin you will conceive; as a virgin you will give birth, as a virgin you will nourish."

Pseudo-Bonaventure

This name is given to many unidentified authors of thirteenth-century works that are attributed to St. Bonaventure. The author of the *Meditations on the Life of Christ* or *The Mirror on the Blessed Life of Jesus Christ*, which appeared at the end of the thirteenth century or the start of the fourteenth century and was influenced by St. Francis of Assisi, embellished the apocryphal writings by discarding what was fantastical in them to imagine what Joseph's ordinary life was like with Jesus and Mary.

We read, "When she was fourteen, the Blessed Virgin Mary married Joseph through a divine inspiration." In regard to Elizabeth's Visitation, the author writes that Mary goes from Nazareth to Elizabeth's home with Joseph, her husband.

This document explains Joseph's mission in these words:

> If, at first, you ask why the Lord wanted his mother to have a husband, since he had decreed that she would always remain a virgin, there are three answers to give you. It was, first of all, in order that her pregnancy would not dishonor her in the eyes of the world. Then, it was to enable her to enjoy society and the protection of a husband. Finally, it was to hide the Son of God's birth from the devil.

When Joseph discovers that his wife is pregnant, doubt enters him:

> As Our Lady and Joseph, her spouse, lived together and the child was growing in his mother's womb, Joseph recognized that Mary was pregnant and

became sorry beyond measure. Joseph looked at his wife and was grieved and troubled. He had a sorrowful look on his face when he saw her and turned his eyes away from her, as if she were to blame. In fact, he suspected her of adultery. Joseph thought about secretly repudiating her.

But once reassured by the angel, he surrounds his wife "with chaste affection more tender than we can say." With her he takes infinite care, and Our Lady stays by his side in the midst of the sweetest confidence. Both of them experience the joy of their poverty. In Bethlehem, they have to "withdraw into a kind of cave where people took shelter. Joseph, who was a master carpenter, presumably made a type of fence there."

These *Meditations* were behind a whole movement of devout literature, whose main representative was Ludolph the Carthusian. Jean de Caulibus, a Franciscan from the fifteenth century, was also described as a pseudo-Bonaventure. In his *Meditations*, he offers three reasons for the marriage of Mary and Joseph: 1) So that, having become pregnant, her reputation would not be subject to any scourge; 2) So that she could be helped by the services of this husband and that he would be a companion to her; and 3) So that the devil would be unaware of the Son of God's Incarnation."

Pseudo-Origen

This unknown author from the fourth century, identified by some people as Gregory of Elvira or Adamantius, delivered a homily for the vigil of the Nativity. In it, he said that Joseph planned to repudiate Mary because he was aware of his unworthiness for having approached the divine mystery—it was a manifestation of his humility. The author refused to accept that Joseph could have suspected Mary of adultery, as Chrysostom or Augustine thought.

Islam and St. Joseph

Since it is based on apocryphal writings, let us say a word here about what Islam thinks of Joseph and Mary.

Mary plays an important role in Islam. Muslims believe that the Quran is a miraculous text that comes directly from God through the intervention of the angel of revelation. The message regarding Mary resembles the apocryphal writings—especially the childhood stories, the *Protoevangelium of James*, the *Gospel of the Nativity of Mary*, the *Gospel of Pseudo-Matthew*, the *Story of Joseph the Carpenter*, and the *Arabic Infancy Gospel*. There is no reference, however, to the canonical Gospels.

The Quran is silent about Joseph's intervention in Mary's life. Yet, the Muslim tradition knows about Joseph and his relations with the Virgin Mary. In it she introduces him as her devotional companion in the temple. It is later that, after contact with the canonical Gospels and the apocryphal writings, that great historians, including Ibn Khaldun, allude to "Joseph the carpenter," the "reunion of the sons of Aaron," the dove that, according to the legend, came out of Joseph's rod, and the responsibility that Joseph took on by judging that the Virgin Mary "appeared to be a wife" (*chibh zaoujah*). After noticing that the Annunciation had taken place, Joseph is said to have been afraid of being falsely accused by the priests, who had entrusted Mary to him so that she would be "like his wife" and not become his wife. However, we do not find any trace of this insinuation, which was reported by Ibn Khaldun, in the Quran. Joseph was not the subject of any suspicion; on the other hand, Zachariah was blamed and had to flee. After listening to his conscience, Joseph took care of Mary and led her into Egypt.

Thus, in the Quran, Mary is a "woman who preserved her virginity" (21:91, 66:12). She is a role model for the believers, one "of those who fear God" (66:12). She is "one of the four best women" who ever existed, along with Aïcha, Khadija, and Fatima. In the Quran we find a tracing of the *Protoevangelium of James*. Mary is led to the temple at the age of three, placed under the authority of the priest Zachariah. An ascetic carpenter named Joseph takes care of her needs and lives with her honorably, "as if they were already married." Mary becomes pregnant and says to Zachariah that "this is coming from the Lord. He provides for whomever he wants, without counting."

Joseph accepts God's will and leads Mary into Egypt. After that, there are the episodes of the Presentation in the Temple, the finding of Jesus when he was twelve years old, and the miracle at Cana. But Jesus is not crucified. He escapes the pursuit of the Jews (who are the object of severe commentary), and is taken up to heaven.

The miracles surrounding Mary's conception, birth, and childhood make up a remote preparation for the role that God reserved for Mary. The Muslim tradition would admit that there was such a preparation, was based on the texts of the Quran. Thus, when Mary goes to draw water with Joseph, the angels come before her saying, "O Mary, God chose you, purified you, and selected you above the world's women" (3:41). Mary sees a messenger appear while she goes looking for water in the spring's cave. In another version, Mary had stepped aside to purify herself. The angel appears to her in human form; some people maintain that he looked like Joseph. He was none other than Gabriel to whom Islam gives a very important role in religious history. This apparition occurred when Mary took back her clothes after thoroughly purifying herself.

The Quran offers some rare details about the Nativity. After having withdrawn toward the East, Mary is gripped by labor pains at the foot of a palm tree. She is so anxious that she wants to die. God then offers her tangible and miraculous consolation by speaking to her through the angel or through Jesus, according to different viewpoints. He orders her to shake the trunk of the palm tree to make dates fall from it. He even brings forth a nearby spring and invites Mary to be joyful and to stay silent before men.

The exegetes commented on and amplified these accounts. They seem, however, to favor the story in which Mary, through a warning from God that makes her foresee the persecution by her own people is led by Joseph toward Egypt on a donkey. The child would be born in a donkey's manger. But this tradition, drowned out in a great variety of stories, was not able to prevail. The commentators did not ask themselves about Christ's miraculous birth. One opinion, more popular than theological, wanted his birth to have occurred in an ordinary way. We find traces of this in Spain during a discussion that St. Ignatius had with a Moor. The saint wished to pursue and kill him because he did not accept the virginity *in partu*.[4]

The testimony of her newborn son, whose innocence is miraculously restored while "speaking in the cradle" is, for Muslims, the most important event in Mary's life after the Nativity. According to some commentators, Mary stayed in a cave for forty days after Jesus' birth while Joseph cared for her. Others think that she met her family. Jesus "spoke in the cradle" before them to exonerate his mother of every accusation. This cradle, say the exegetes, is the arms of Mary, for she had neither a home nor a cradle to offer her son.

---

4 The belief that Mary remained a virgin before, during, and after Christ's birth.

PART IV

St. Joseph

and the

Popes

Excerpts of Pontifical and Conciliar Comments About St. Joseph

Siricius of Rome (384–399)

In 392, he wrote to Anysius of Thessalonica:

> Surely, we cannot deny that regarding the sons of Mary the statement is justly censured, and your holiness has rightly abhorred it, that from the same virginal womb, from which according to the flesh Christ was born, another offspring was brought forth. For neither would the Lord Jesus have chosen to be born of a virgin, if he had judged she would be so incontinent that with the seed of human copulation she would pollute that generative chamber of the Lord's body, that palace of the eternal king.

Sixtus IV (1471–1484)

On March 19, 1476, he put the Feast of St. Joseph into the Roman breviary.

Innocent VIII (1484–1492)

Raised the Office of St. Joseph to the double rite in 1486.

Gregory XV (1621–1623)

In responding to Isidore of Isolanis's wish, he extended the Feast of St. Joseph to the whole Catholic world. He made it mandatory as of May 8, 1621. But the decree was not applied everywhere outside of Italy.

Urban VIII (1623–1644)

Renewed Gregory XV's decision to make the Feast of St. Joseph mandatory.

Clement X (1670–1676)

Raised the Feast of St. Joseph to a second-class rite in 1670.

Innocent XI (1676–1689)

Responded favorably to the Carmelites' petitions to have St. Joseph be their order's patron. He also granted them their own liturgy, which was celebrated on the third Sunday of Easter.

Clement XI (1700–1721)

Completed the *Te Joseph celebrant*, and raised the Feast of St. Joseph to a second-class double rite. He completely reformed the Office of St. Joseph. In 1714, he also approved three hymns of the Office of St. Joseph, which were composed by the Spanish Carmelite Fray Juan Escollar (1621-1700).

Benedict XIII (1724–1730)

In 1726, he extended the Feast of the Espousal of St. Joseph to the entire Church and put St. Joseph in the *Litany of the Saints*.

Benedict XIV (1740–1758)

Relying on St. Augustine, he wrote that "St. Joseph belongs to the saints of the New Testament. On the other hand, John the Baptist belongs to the saints of the Old Testament, whose list he closes. Likewise, Mary and Joseph start the series of saints in the New Testament." In the *Dissertation on St. Joseph*, Benedict asserted that "St. Joseph was called the patron of the Church Militant by one of his most enthusiastic panegyrists. May his prayers succeed in having God grant peace to the Church and the conversion of all those who are in the wrong."

Pius VI *(1775–1799)*
On May 31, 1783, he had a Polish icon of the Holy Family crowned in Kalisz (Poland).

Pius VII *(1800–1823)*
The pope who had important and painful quarrels with Napoleon also, on September 17, 1815, added the name of St. Joseph, after the Virgin Mary's name, to the prayer *A cunctis*.

Gregory XVI *(1831–1846)*
On January 22, 1836, he granted particular indulgences to the faithful who practiced the devotion of the Seven Sorrows and Seven Joys of St. Joseph in support of the sick.

Pius IX *(1846–1878)*
Very devoted to St. Joseph, on March 22, 1847, he granted particular indulgences, via a decree of the Sacred Congregation of Indulgences and Holy Relics, to the faithful who practiced the Seven Sundays Devotion in honor of the Seven Sorrows and Seven Joys of St. Joseph. On the following December 10, he established the liturgy for the patronage of St. Joseph (decree of the Sacred Congregation of Rites *Inclytus Patriarcha Joseph*).

In 1854, he declared that Joseph was, after Mary, the Church's sure hope. In 1859, he approved the blessing of the White Cord of St. Joseph, whose devotion spread in Belgium. In 1865, he dedicated the month of March to St. Joseph and granted a number of graces and indulgences on this occasion.

During Vatican I (1869-1870), Pius IX received a petition

that was signed by 153 bishops who were asking that the cult of St. Joseph play a more important role in the holy liturgy. Another document, which was signed by forty-three superiors from religious orders, asked that Joseph be proclaimed as the patron of the universal Church. On April 27, 1865, through an *Urbi et Orbi* decree, the Roman pontiff connected the month of Mary's indulgences to the month of March, which was dedicated to St. Joseph.

On December 8, 1870—on the day dedicated to the Immaculate Virgin Mary, the mother of God, and the wife of the most chaste Joseph—the Sacred Congregation of Rites promulgated *Quemadmodum Deus* [see below], which communicated Pius's decision to make Joseph patron of the universal Church and raised his March 19 feast to a solemnity. This important act was confirmed by the apostolic letter *Inclytum Patriarcham* on July 7, 1871. It was a true little treatise on Joseph, in which the pontiff stressed the patriarch's titles, grandeur, dignity, holiness, and mission. This made it possible for Joseph to have the right to a veneration that was superior to that of the other saints, since to Joseph God had accorded special graces.

Pius IX wanted Francesco Podesti's spectacular fresco in the Column of the Immaculate Conception in Rome, which reminds us of the definition and proclamation of the dogma of Mary's Immaculate Conception, also to represent Joseph, inserted between St. Peter and Jesus.

Leo XIII *(1878–1903)*

In his first speech to the College of Cardinals on March 28, 1878, Leo XIII placed his pontificate under the powerful protection of St. Joseph, the Church's heavenly patron. He repeated it in his first encyclical, *Inscrutabili Dei Consilio*, on April 21, 1878. He ended the encyclical *Aeterni Patris*, on August 4, 1879, by asking for prayers to "blessed Joseph, the

Virgin Mary's most pure husband." In the apostolic letter *Militans Iesu Christi Ecclesia*, on March 12, 1881, he entrusted the extraordinary jubilee, which was to start on Joseph's feast day, to him. In 1883, he approved the Mass and votive office for each Wednesday, via a July 5 *Urbi et Orbi* decree.

In the encyclical *Quamquam Pluries*, on August 15, 1889, he expounded on the teachings about St. Joseph from the basis for his dignity up to the unique reason for which he deserved to be proclaimed as the patron of the whole Church and the model and advocate of all Christian families. Through the apostolic letter *Quod Paucis Abhinc*, on January 28, 1890, he let Spain and its colonies celebrate the Feast of St. Joseph as a day of precept. In the apostolic letter *Quod Erat* on March 3, 1891, Leo XIII confirmed that, in order to preserve the heritage of faith and live as Christians, nothing was more efficient than gaining Joseph's support and obtaining favors for the faithful from Mary, the mother of God, through her chaste spouse.

Finally, the apostolic letter *Neminem Fugit*, on June 14, 1892, maintained that Joseph intimately participated in the Holy Family's supreme dignity. In this letter, we read that

> to all fathers of families, Joseph is verily the best model of paternal vigilance and care. In the most holy virgin mother of God, mothers may find an excellent example of love, modesty, resignation of spirit, and the perfecting of faith. And in Jesus, who was subject to his parents, the children of the family have a divine pattern of obedience which they can admire, reverence, and imitate.

Another *Urbi et Orbi* decree, on August 15, 1892, determined that if the Feast of St. Joseph fell on Passion Sunday, it would be celebrated on the following Monday. If it coincided with Holy Week, it would be celebrated on the Wednesday after the *in albis* Sunday.[5] Leo XIII granted to having the Feast of the Holy Family on the third Sunday after Epiphany via a decree of the Sacred Congregation of Rites on July 21, 1893.

In the encyclical *Quamquam Pluries*, Leo XIII intended to encourage Christians "to continually invoke with great piety and trust God, together with the virgin mother of God, her chaste spouse, the blessed Joseph; and we regard it as most certain that this will be most pleasing to the virgin herself." This devotion had already been dispersed among the people of God, thanks to the action of many Roman pontiffs. But it must "engraft itself upon the daily pious practice of Catholics. We desire that the Christian people should be urged to it above all by our words and authority."

Leo XIII offered the main reasons for this:

> Joseph was the spouse of Mary and he was reputed as the father of Jesus Christ. From these sources have sprung his dignity, his holiness, his glory. . . As Joseph has been united to the Blessed Virgin by the ties of marriage, it may not be doubted that he approached nearer than any to the eminent dignity by which the mother of God surpasses so nobly all created natures . . .
>
> Thus in giving Joseph the Blessed Virgin as spouse, God appointed him to be not only her life's companion, the witness of her maidenhood, the protector of her honor, but also, by virtue of the conjugal tie, a participator in her sublime dignity . . . Thus, Joseph was, by divine will, the guardian of the Son of God and reputed as his father among

---

5 White Sunday, the second Sunday of Easter.

men. Hence it came about that the Word of God was humbly subject to Joseph, that he obeyed him, and that he rendered to him all those offices that children are bound to render to their parents.

Joseph fulfilled those charges and those duties that nature lays upon the head of families. He set himself to protect with a mighty love and a daily solicitude his spouse and the divine infant; regularly by his work he earned what was necessary for the one and the other for nourishment and clothing; he guarded from death the child threatened by a monarch's jealousy and found for him a refuge; in the miseries of the journey and in the bitternesses of exile he was ever the companion, the assistance, and the upholder of the Virgin and of Jesus. Now the divine house that Joseph ruled with the authority of a father contained within its limits the scarce-born Church. . . . It is, then, natural and worthy that as the blessed Joseph ministered to all the needs of the family at Nazareth and girt it about with his protection, he should now cover with the cloak of his heavenly patronage and defend the Church of Jesus Christ.

The Church admits that the "Joseph of ancient times, son of the patriarch Jacob, was the type of St. Joseph, and the former by his glory prefigured the greatness of the future guardian of the Holy Family. Men of every rank and country should fly to the trust and guard of the blessed Joseph. Fathers of families find in Joseph the best personification of paternal solicitude and vigilance; spouses a perfect example of love, of peace, and of conjugal fidelity; virgins at the same time find in him the model and protector of virginal integrity. The noble of birth will learn of Joseph how to guard their dignity even in misfortune; the rich will understand, by his lessons, what are the goods most to be desired and won at the price of their labor.

As to workmen, artisans, and persons of lesser degree, their recourse to Joseph is a special right, and his example is for their particular imitation. For Joseph, of royal blood, united by marriage to the greatest and holiest of women, reputed as the father of the Son of God, passed his life in labor. . . . Joseph, content with his slight possessions, bore the trials consequent on a fortune so slender, with greatness of soul, in imitation of his son, who subjected himself of his own free will to the spoliation and loss of everything.

Joseph is truly the model of all those who live by the work of their hands. The encyclical of Leo XIII concludes with these words:

We prescribe that during the whole month of October, at the recitation of the rosary . . . a prayer to St. Joseph be added, and that this custom should be repeated every year . . . It is a salutary practice and very praiseworthy . . . to consecrate the month of March to the honor of the holy patriarch by daily exercises of piety. . . . We exhort the faithful to sanctify the nineteenth of March as far as possible by private pious practices, in honor of their heavenly patron.

Leo XIII also composed a prayer, which includes indulgences, that is intended to be recited with the rosary during the month of the rosary. In addition, he is the author of the prayer *Ad Te Beate Joseph*.

Pius X *(1903–1914)*

St. Pius approved the decree of the Sacred Congregation of Rites that published St. Joseph's litanies. On March 18, 1909, this *Urbi et Orbi* decree explained the pope's intervention with these words: "Our Holy Father Pius X has always been very devoted to the noble St. Joseph, who was the divine Redeemer's putative father, the most pure spouse of the Virgin mother of God, and the powerful patron of the Catholic Church with God, whose glorious name he received in baptism."

Pius X also composed a prayer to the glorious Joseph, model of workers:

> Glorious St. Joseph, model of all who are devoted to labor, obtain for me the grace to work in the spirit of penance in expiation of my many sins;
>
> To work conscientiously by placing love of duty above my inclinations;
>
> To gratefully and joyfully deem it an honor to employ and to develop by labor the gifts I have received from God;
>
> To work methodically, peacefully, and in moderation and patience, without ever shrinking from it through weariness or difficulty to work;
>
> Above all, with purity of intention and unselfishness, having unceasingly before my eyes death and the account I have to render time lost, talents unused, good not done, and vain complacency in success, so baneful to the work of God.
>
> All for Jesus, all for Mary, all to imitate thee, O patriarch St. Joseph! This shall be my motto for life and eternity. Amen.

The supreme pontiff moved the Feast of St. Joseph, patron of the universal Church, from the third Sunday of Easter to the following Wednesday. On July 24, 1911, by decree he modified some feasts of St. Joseph as well as their liturgical rank. He ordered the saint's litanies to be prepared.

Benedict XV *(1914–1922)*

On April 9, 1919, Benedict published several prefaces that were intended for Masses in honor of St. Joseph. On July 25, 1920, during the fiftieth anniversary of the proclamation of Joseph's patronage over the whole Church, he published a *motu proprio* called *Bonum Sane*, in which, after having recalled the moral distress that was caused by the recent Great War, he wrote:

> Concerned . . . to keep the men who earn their bread with labor immune from the contagion of socialism, the bitter enemy of Christian principles. We with great solicitude offer them in a particular way St. Joseph—that they might follow him as their special guide and honor him as their heavenly patron. He, in fact, lived a life similar to theirs, so much so that Jesus, God, despite being the Only Begotten of the Eternal Father, willed to be called "the carpenter's son." But he knew how to adorn that humble and poor condition of his with so much and so many types of virtue! Above all, those virtues were to shine in the spouse of Mary Immaculate, and in the putative father of our Lord Jesus.

Benedict XV named St. Joseph as the special patron of the dying. He invited the bishops to offer their support to "those pious associations instituted to supplicate Joseph in favor of the dying, such as "Of a happy Death," the "Transit of St. Joseph," and "For the Dying" because he is justly held as the most efficacious protector of the dying, having expired with the assistance of Jesus and Mary."

In an *Urbi et Orbi* decree of February 23, 1921, Benedict Joseph's name in the anti-blasphemous acclamations that were said at the end of the greeting to the Blessed Sacrament.

Pius XI *(1922–1939)*

On April 21, 1926, during the beatification of two blessed French people—André Hubert Fournet (1752-1834), founder of the Sisters of the Cross, and Jeanne-Antide Thouret (1765-1826), founder of the Daughters of Charity—Pius explained, in regard to St. Joseph:

> Here is a saint who enters into life and works hard at accomplishing an incomparable divine mission: to keep Mary pure, to protect our Lord; to hide, through his admirable cooperation, the mystery— the secret that everyone is unaware of, with the exception of the Most Holy Trinity—of the redemption of humankind. St. Joseph's unique and absolutely incomparable holiness is rooted in this mission's greatness, since such a mission was not really entrusted to any other soul, to any other saint. Between St. Joseph and God, we only see and are only able to see the Most Blessed Virgin Mary with her divine motherhood. It is evident that, by virtue of this very high mission, this holy patriarch already had the title of glory that was his: that of the patron of the universal Church . . . The Church was already present, around St. Joseph, when he discharged his duty as the Holy Family's father and guardian.

On March 19, 1928, during the reading of the decree on the heroic virtues of Jeanne-Élisabeth Bichier des Anges (1773–1838), the founder of the Sisters of the Cross, Pius XI declared:

St. Joseph's mission occurred between the missions of John the Baptist and Peter. It was a contemplative and silent mission that was almost unnoticed at the time and would only be illuminated a few centuries later. The silence was to be followed much later by a resounding song of glory. The mission is the loftiest when the mystery is the deepest, the night that covers it the darkest, and the silence the greatest. The series of virtues and merits that are required for this type of mission are the most brilliant. These merits must echo the virtues.

It is a unique mission, a high and great mission, to cooperate with the Incarnation.

On March 19, 1937, in the encyclical *Divini Redemptoris*, Pius XI indicated: "We place the vast campaign of the Church against world Communism under the standard of St. Joseph, her mighty protector." He added that

Joseph belongs to the working class, and he bore the burdens of poverty for himself and the Holy Family, whose tender and vigilant head he was. To him was entrusted the divine child when Herod hurled his assassins against him. In a life of faithful performance of everyday duties, he left an example for all who might gain their bread by the toil of their hands. He won for himself the title of "the Just," serving thus as a living model of that Christian justice that should reign in social life.

Finally, in his Allocution to Married Couples on March 19, 1938, Pius XI recognized that "as St. Joseph was really the head or master of the home, his intercession cannot help but be omnipotent."

Pius XII (1939–1958)

On April 10, 1940, in a speech to young couples on St. Joseph's admirable example, Pius expressed himself in these terms:

> How can we, in welcoming you, dear couples, not turn our thought toward St. Joseph, the Virgin Mary's most chaste spouse, and the patron of the universal Church, whose solemnity the Church celebrates today? If all Christians resort to this glorious patriarch's protection for a good reason, you certainly are especially qualified to do this . . .
>
> The rare and brief passages in the Gospel that talk about him are enough to show what a good head of the family, model, and special patron he is for you, young couples, as a result.
>
> Joseph was faithful about the task that God had entrusted to him in regard to Mary and the divine child. He especially watched over their physical life. When, in obeying Augustus's edict, he went to be registered in the Bethlehem census, he did not want to leave Mary, who was to become the mother of God, alone in Nazareth.
>
> In the absence of details in the evangelical accounts, devout souls like to imagine more deeply the care that he then lavished on the Virgin Mary and her divine child. They see him lifting the inn's solid door . . . and talking, in vain, to his relatives and friends. In the end, after having gotten discouraged everywhere, he strived, at least, to organize and clean the cave. He held Jesus' cold little trembling hands in his manly hands to warm them up.
>
> Having learned a little later that his treasure was threatened, "he took the child and his mother

by night" (Matt. 2:14). He led them into Egypt, through sandy trails, while removing stones and brambles from the path. He worked hard to feed them. Heaven ordered him, probably a few years after his arrival, to go to Galilee, at the price of the same pains. In Nazareth (Matt. 2:22-23), Joseph showed Jesus, his divine apprentice, how to handle a saw and a plane. He sometimes left his home to go work outside. When he returned in the evening, Jesus and Mary were waiting for him on the doorstep and smiled at him. He sat with them around a small table for a simple meal.

A family man's most urgent task is to provide bread for his wife and children, Oh! How sad he is when he sees those he loves languish because there is nothing more in the cupboard or purse!

But Providence led the first Joseph by the hand when he was betrayed by his brothers, first made a slave, then superintendent and the overseer of all of Egypt (Gen. 41:43) and then his own family's provider (45:18). God led the second Joseph into the same region, where he arrived stripped of everything. He did not know the residents, their customs, or language. Yet, he safely returned from there with Mary and was still active. And Jesus increased in wisdom and in years, and in grace (Luke 2:52).

Knowing how to ask God for what we need is the secret of prayer and its power. This is another one of St. Joseph's teachings. It is true that the Gospel does not specifically tell us what prayers were said in the home in Nazareth. But the Holy Family's faithfulness to religious practices was explicitly confirmed for us, if it was ever needed, when St. Luke (2:41 *et seq.*) told us that, according to the custom, Jesus went to the temple in Jerusalem for the Easter festivities with Mary and Joseph. Thus, it is sweet to imagine the Holy Family when they were praying.

When speaking to members of the Italian Catholic Action in 1947, he recommended this to them:

> There has never been a man who was so close to the Redeemer through domestic ties, daily relationships, spiritual harmony, and the divine life of grace than Joseph, who was from David's race, and, nonetheless, a humble manual laborer. . . . How would you not have chosen him as your heavenly patron?

After hosting the conference of the Christian Associations of Italian workers on May 1, 1955, Pius XII established the Feast of St. Joseph the Worker. It had its own proper Mass and office, and martyrological text, which was intended to replace the text about the patronage of St. Joseph:

> There could be no better protector to help you have the spirit of the Gospel pervade your lives . . . It is certain that no worker was so perfectly and deeply filled with it than Jesus' putative father. Jesus lived with him most intimately in a family and work community. Likewise, if you want to be adopted by Christ, we repeat this to you again: go to Joseph. . . . We are pleased to tell you about our determination to establish—as we do so in reality—the liturgical Feast of Joseph the Worker, by having it be in May.

The institution of this feast was accompanied by a new liturgy that included its own Mass and office.

On May 15, 1956, in the encyclical *Haurietis Aquas in Gaudio*, the pope described the intimate relationship that Jesus had with Joseph: "The adorable heart of Jesus Christ began to beat with a love at once human and divine when in the house of Nazareth he conversed with his most sweet mother and his foster father, St. Joseph, in obedience to whom he performed laborious tasks in the trade of a carpenter."

On March 11, 1958, the public Sacred Apostolic Penitentiary published a prayer of Pius XII to St. Joseph, which carried many indulgences.

John XXIII (1958–1963)

He initiated the Second Vatican Council and was canonized in 2014 by Pope Francis. During a homily that he gave on May 26, 1960, John XXIII accepted St. Bernardino of Siena's idea, which was taken up again by St. Francis de Sales, that St. Joseph and St. John the Baptist are included among the saints who rose with Christ and entered heaven with him during his Ascension.

In the apostolic letter *Le Voci*, March 19, 1961, John recalled the steady growth of the cult of St. Joseph. He summarized the actions of the preceding pontiffs in honor of St. Joseph and named him protector of the Second Vatican Council. Joseph is again mentioned in the apostolic exhortation *Sacra Laudis*, which was issued on January 6, 1962.

On November 13, 1962, John announced a *motu proprio* to the Council Fathers, through the intervention of the cardinal secretary of state, his decision to insert the name of St. Joseph in the *Communicantes* prayer at Mass. That same day, a decree of the Sacred Congregation of Rites indeed inserted the name of St. Joseph into the Eucharistic prayer memorial in the Roman Canon:

> *Infra actionem post verba: Communicantes . . .*
> *Domini nostri Jesu Christi, haec addantur:*
> *sed et beati Joseph eiusdem Virginia sponsi.*

John XIII thus responded favorably to many requests and petitions, the first ones going back to 1815, including that of Fr. Cyprien Macabiau, S.J. A memorandum of seventy-five pages, which came from the Oratory in Montreal and the centers for Josephology in Valladolid and Viterbe, had been sent to the world's bishops in 1961, along with a petition for this purpose.

Paul VI (1963–1978)

Also canonized by Pope Francis, in 2018. In his homily of March 19, 1965, Paul VI exalted St. Joseph's simplicity and humility:

> Joseph's modesty was the most popular, common, and ordinary kind that there was, according to the term that is used for human values since we cannot find anything in him that can offer us a reason for his greatness and the extraordinary mission that God entrusted to him. It is the legitimate theme of so many opinions—even speeches in honor of St. Joseph. . . . Joseph seemed to us to be very humble. He was a modest and obscure worker, who was not at all unusual. His words are not in the Gospels.

Paul emphasized Joseph's silent reserve and perfect obedience:

> Joseph was always a remarkable unrivaled guardian, assistant, and teacher. He was amazingly great because of his total and obedient devotion. . . . As we easily trust a saint who does not know how to intimidate you and does not place any distance between himself and us, and who even, with a confounding condescension, is at our feet, so to speak:

see the grade that was assigned to me! Jesus chose Joseph. . . . He chose the humblest and simplest instrument as his collaborator. In a way, He manifested Jesus' exclusive power of redemption.

The pontiff pointed out God's own condescension and goodness toward humankind. He emphasized that God

made himself very small . . . the Lord came down to the last place on the social ladder. What joy the humble, the poor, sinners, and disadvantaged people experience—those who are fully aware of human misery . . . How they revel in being introduced to Christ by a guardian and patron like St. Joseph ! . . . St. Joseph illustrates the cry that we should hear as one of the most expressive ones in the gospel: "Come to me, all you that are weary and are carrying heavy burdens, and I will give you rest."

Paul VI returned to Joseph in his March 19, 1968 homily in which he exalted the humility of the Incarnation and paid tribute to the one who carried out God's will; the following year, highlighting St. Joseph's poor and hidden life; and March 19, 1975, highlighting Joseph's unique situation.

In a letter to Cardinal Villot, on November 25, 1970, which was written during a national symposium in Rome, Paul VI encouraged research on St. Joseph in order to "understand and appreciate the unique position that God gave Joseph, in union with Mary, his wife, in the mystery of Christ and the Church."

In 1965, a canonical crowning of a statue of St. Joseph occurred in the first convent of St. Teresa of Ávila's Carmelite reform. In 1969, Paul VI moved the Feast of the Holy Family to the Sunday after the Nativity.

John Paul II *(1978–2005)*

This Polish pope, after having brought the Church into Christianity's third millennium, was beatified by Benedict XVI and canonized by Pope Francis in 2014. In a homily on March 19, 1982, he stated that St. Joseph's holiness was, first of all, to be found in his heroic, unshakeable faith: "He had a strong faith, not because he spoke his own words, but, above all, because he listened to the voice of the living God. St. Joseph always listened to the Word of God."

In his March 19, 1986 homily, John Paul II set up a parallel between human and divine fatherhood. "The interior space of the vocation that comes from God himself expands in a child's soul in the atmosphere of the parents' care." Human fatherhood "restores man to God—God's very fatherhood."

In a homily on May 1, 1988, John Paul came back to the theme of the dignity of work and its redeeming value. Joseph was a worker—a craftsman:

> He invited workers—better yet—he authoritatively summoned them to find—like him and with him—their place near Jesus, who was known by his contemporaries as "the carpenter's son" . . . The work and those who did it have entered into the history of salvation, that is to say, in this work that Jesus came to accomplish for us in this world. He did this, first of all, in his carpentry work, and then in his ministry as a preacher and performer of miracles. In the end, he did it through his resurrection.

On August 15, 1989, John Paul II published the apostolic exhortation known as *Redemptoris Custos* during the centennial of the publication of Pope Leo XIII's encyclical *Quamquam Pluries*. "Joseph was called to look after the Redeemer," he wrote. "He did as the angel of the Lord commanded him: he took his wife into his home" (1). Thus, Joseph's vocation was to watch over Jesus and his mother. His primary virtue was obedience. He did what the angel asked him to do. He became the model of husbands and, therefore, of fathers and, thereby, the founder of holy families and the model of the heads of households. Joseph behaved like the guardian of God's mystery and Jesus' father in the eyes of men.

Like Mary, we can say about him: "Blessed is she who believed." Obeying in faith, "he did as the angel commanded him" (4). He

> is the first to share in the faith of the mother of God and that in doing so he supports his spouse in the faith of the divine annunciation. He is also the first to be placed by God on the path of Mary's pilgrimage of faith. It is a path along which—especially at the time of Calvary and Pentecost—Mary will precede in a perfect way" (5).

Joseph's fatherhood comes to pass through Mary, that is, through the family (7). And although it is important for the Church to profess the virginal conception of Jesus, it is not less important to uphold Mary's marriage to Joseph, because juridically Joseph's fatherhood depends on it. Hence, the importance of reading Joseph's genealogy. St. Joseph was called by God to serve the person and mission of Jesus through the exercise of his fatherhood over the Holy Family. He cooperated "in the fullness of time in the great mystery of salvation . . . He made his life a service, a sacrifice to the mystery of the Incarnation and to the redemptive mission connected with it. . . . God placed him at the head of his family, as a faithful servant and prudent servant, so that with fatherly care he might watch over his only begotten Son."

All of Jesus' "private" or "hidden" life was entrusted to Joseph's care (8). Joseph also appears as the just man and the husband. Joseph's life, like Mary's, was a pilgrimage in the faith, in fidelity to God, humility, and silence. Mary and Joseph were united by a spousal and virginal love. These two loves together represent "the mystery of the Church, virgin and spouse, of which the marriage of Mary and Joseph is a symbol . . . . Joseph, at the express command of the angel, takes Mary into his home and respects her exclusive belonging to God."

"Joseph expressed love through his work. Thanks to Joseph, human work took on a special emphasis in the Gospel. This work entered into the mystery of the Incarnation at the same time as the Son of God's humanity." And the "submission or obedience of Jesus in the house of Nazareth should be understood as sharing in the work of Joseph" (22). St. Joseph, the model of those humble ones that Christianity raises up to great destinies, definitively sanctified his daily life (24).

The pope then turns to St. Joseph's interior life. He lived in an atmosphere of deep contemplation. The relationship of Jesus and Joseph was completely unique and Joseph "is a luminous example of the interior life." In Joseph, the union of the active life and contemplative life reached its perfection. "We can say that Joseph experienced the love of the divine truth that radiated from Christ's humanity as well as the demand of love, that is to say, the pure love of service, which is required for the protection and development of this same humanity (27).

St. John Paul II wanted the third millennium to be specifically placed under the patronage of Mary's husband and Jesus Christ's reputed father. "This patronage must be invoked as ever necessary for the Church . . . primarily, as an impetus for her renewed commitment to evangelization in the world . . . . Besides trusting in Joseph's sure protection, the Church also trusts in his noble example . . . which serves a model for the entire Christian community" (29).

Benedict XVI (2005–2013)

The Bavarian Cardinal Joseph Ratzinger, prefect for the Congregation for the Doctrine of the Faith for twenty years, was elected pope in 2005, to succeed St. John Paul II. "May Mary, the Star of Evangelization," he wrote in a July 16, 2012 message, "and her chaste spouse Joseph, intercede so that the 'star' that the Lord has lit in the universe—the Church, with St. Teresa's reform, would continue to radiate the great splendor of Christ's love and truth to all men."

In his December 18, 2005 Angelus, he taught:

> Today, I would like to turn my gaze to the figure of St. Joseph. In today's Gospel, St. Luke presents the Virgin Mary as "betrothed to a man whose name was Joseph, of the house of David" (Luke 1:27). The evangelist Matthew, however, places a greater emphasis on the putative father of Jesus, stressing that through him, the child belonged legally to the lineage of David and thus fulfilled the scriptural prophecy that the Messiah would be "a son of David."
>
> But Joseph's role cannot be reduced to this legal aspect. He was the model of a "righteous" man (Matt. 1:19) who, in perfect harmony with his wife, welcomed the Son of God made man and watched over his human growth. It is therefore particularly appropriate in the days that precede Christmas to establish a sort of spiritual conversation with St. Joseph so that he may help us to live to the full this great mystery of faith . . . .

His silence is steeped in contemplation of the mystery of God in an attitude of total availability to the divine desires. In other words, St. Joseph's silence does not express an inner emptiness but, on the contrary, the fullness of the faith he bears in his heart and which guides his every thought and action. It is a silence to which Joseph, in unison with Mary, watches over the Word of God, known through the sacred scriptures, continuously comparing it with the events of the life of Jesus; a silence woven of constant prayer, a prayer of blessing of the Lord, of the adoration of his holy will and of unreserved entrustment to his providence.

It is no exaggeration to think that it was precisely from "his father" Joseph that Jesus learned—at the human level—that steadfast interiority that is a presupposition of authentic justice, the "superior justice" that he was one day to teach his disciples (cf. Matt. 5:20).

Francis (elected 2013)

Pope Francis took over his office on March 19, the Solemnity of St. Joseph who is present in his pontifical wardrobe in the form of a nard flower called the "flower of St. Joseph." Francis dedicated the entire homily of his installation on the throne of St. Peter to the figure of St. Joseph:

> I thank the Lord that I can celebrate this Holy Mass for the inauguration of my Petrine ministry on the Solemnity of St. Joseph, the spouse of the Virgin Mary and the patron of the universal Church. It is a significant coincidence, and it is also the name-day of my venerable predecessor: we are close to him with our prayers, full of affection and gratitude. In

the Gospel we heard that "Joseph did as the angel of the Lord commanded him and took Mary as his wife" (Matt. 1:24). These words already point to the mission that God entrusts to Joseph: he is to be the *custos*, the protector . . . .

How does Joseph exercise his role as protector? Discreetly, humbly, and silently, but with an unfailing presence and utter fidelity, even when he finds it hard to understand. From the time of his betrothal to Mary until the finding of the twelve-year-old Jesus in the Temple of Jerusalem, he is there at every moment with loving care. As the spouse of Mary, he is at her side in good times and bad, on the journey to Bethlehem for the census and in the anxious and joyful hours when she gave birth; amid the drama of the flight into Egypt and during the frantic search for their child in the temple; and later in the day-to-day life in the home of Nazareth, in the workshop where he taught his trade to Jesus. How does Joseph respond to his calling to be the protector of Mary, Jesus, and the Church? By being constantly attentive to God, open to the signs of God's presence and receptive to God's plans, and not simply to his own.

This is what God asked of David, as we heard in the first reading. God does not want a house built by men, but faithfulness to his word, to his plan. It is God himself who builds the house, but from living stones sealed by his Spirit. Joseph is a "protector" because he is able to hear God's voice and be guided by his will; and for this reason he is all the more sensitive to the persons entrusted to his safekeeping. He can look at things realistically, he is in touch with his surroundings, he can make truly wise decisions.

In him, dear friends, we learn how to respond to God's call readily and willingly, but we also see the core of the Christian vocation, which is Christ! Let us protect Christ in our lives, so that we can protect others, so that we can protect creation! . . . In the Gospels, St. Joseph appears as a strong and courageous man, a working man, yet in his heart we see great tenderness, which is not the virtue of the weak but rather a sign of strength of spirit and a capacity for concern, for compassion, for genuine openness to others, for love.

In his general audience on March 19, 2014, the pope invited people to look at Joseph

as the model of the educator, who *looked after Jesus in his path of growth "in wisdom and in stature, and in divine and human favor,"* as the Gospel of Luke tells us (2:52). He was not Jesus' father; Jesus' father was God; but he was Jesus' papa. He served as his father to help him grow. And how did he help him grow? In wisdom, in stature, and in grace. . . .

Let us start with *stature*, which is the most natural dimension. Joseph, along with Mary, took care of Jesus, above all, in this area—that is to say, he raised him by taking care that he did not miss what was needed for his healthy development. Let us not forget that this thoughtful care of the child's life also went through the flight into Egypt and the tough experience of living like refugees. Joseph was a refugee, along with Mary and Jesus, to escape Herod's threat. Then, once they returned to their country and settled in Nazareth, Jesus lived a hidden life within the Holy Family for a very long time.

During those years, Joseph taught Jesus his trade, and Jesus learned how to be a carpenter, like his father Joseph. . . .

Let us go on to the second dimension of Jesus' education—that of "wisdom". . . . We can imagine how Joseph educated little Jesus while listening to the holy scriptures—especially when he accompanied Jesus to the synagogue in Nazareth on Saturday. Joseph accompanied him in order for Jesus to listen to the Word of God in the synagogue. Jesus proved to Joseph and Mary how deeply he was listening to God (in a way that was surprising to them) when, at the age of twelve, he stayed in the temple in Jerusalem without their knowing it. He returned after three days, while he was talking with doctors of the law, who were astonished by his *wisdom*. There: Jesus was filled with wisdom, for he was the Son of God. But the Heavenly Father used St. Joseph's collaboration in order that his Son would grow up "filled with wisdom" (Luke 2:40).

Finally, there is the dimension of "grace." St. Luke tells us again, in referring to Jesus: "The favor of God was upon him" (Luke 2:40). Here, the part reserved for St. Joseph is certainly more limited. . . . But it would be a serious mistake to think that a father and mother cannot do anything to raise their children to grow in God's grace. To grow in stature, to grow in wisdom, to grow in grace: this is the work Joseph did with Jesus, to help him grow in these three dimensions. Joseph did this in a unique and matchless way. . . .

In this area of grace, his educational work consisted of assisting the Holy Spirit in Jesus' heart and life, in accordance with the Virgin Mary. This educational area is the more specific one of faith, prayer, adoration, and the acceptance of God's will and his plan. Joseph also raised Jesus through his example, particularly in this dimension of grace. It was the example of a "righteous man" (Matt. 1:19), which lets itself be guided by faith and knows that salvation does not come from the observance of the law, but from God's grace, love, and fidelity.

Pope Francis added the name of "St. Joseph, Mary's spouse" to canons II, III, and IV of the Mass via a decree on May 1, 2013, relying on the doctrine that was announced by St. John Paul II in *Redemptoris Custos*.

POPE FRANCIS'S REMEDY FOR SLEEP

I have great love for St. Joseph, because he is a man of silence and strength. On my table I have an image of St. Joseph sleeping. Even when he is asleep, he is taking care of the Church! Yes! We know that he can do that. So, when I have a problem, a difficulty, I write a little note and I put it underneath St. Joseph, so that he can dream about it! In other words I tell him, "Pray for this problem!". . . Joseph listened to the angel of the Lord and responded to God's call to care for Jesus and Mary. In this way he played his part in God's plan and became a blessing not only for the Holy Family but for all of humanity. With Mary, Joseph served as a model for the boy Jesus as he grew in wisdom, age and grace (Luke 2:52). When families bring children into the world, train them in faith and sound values, and teach them to contribute to society, they become a blessing in our world.[73]

On May 24, 2015, In the encyclical *Laudato Si'* on safe-guarding the common home, Pope Francis wrote that at Mary's side

> in the Holy Family of Nazareth, stands the figure of St. Joseph. Through his work and generous pres-ence, he cared for and defended Mary and Jesus, delivering them from the violence of the unjust by bringing them to Egypt. The gospel presents Joseph as a just man, hard-working and strong. But he also shows great tenderness, which is not a mark of the weak but of those who are genuinely strong, fully aware of reality and ready to love and serve in hu-mility. That is why he was proclaimed custodian of the universal Church. He too can teach us how to show care; he can inspire us to work with generosity and tenderness in protecting this world that God has entrusted to us (242).

First Vatican Council *(1870-1871)*

At the Church's twentieth ecumenical assembly, three *pos-tulata* were presented about St. Joseph's patronage. The first *postulatum*, which was signed by 153 Council fathers, sum-marized the saint's greatness and echoes the universal desire to see his veneration grow. It asked, first of all, that St. Jo-seph, because he was named to be Jesus' father, would, after the Virgin Mary, be honored above all the blessed—that is to say, with reverence greater than the *dulia* given to saints. It also asked that St. Joseph, to whom the Holy Family's care was entrusted, be regarded as the Church's first patron.

The second *postulatum*, which was signed by forty-three vicars-general of different orders, expressed the desire for St. Joseph to be proclaimed as the Church's universal patron. It argued that: 1) It is fitting that the Christian people's patron be none other than Joseph; 2) that the faithful cry out for his patronage; and 3) that the Church and Christ are like one and the same person. Is it not appropriate that the Church would entrust herself specifically to the affectionate care of the one whom Jesus Christ chose as his foster father? Is it not natural that, in order to escape the innumerable traps of her enemies, she would place herself under the auspices of the one who foiled the plans of the elderly Herod against the Savior?

Finally, the third *postulatum*, which was presented by 118 council fathers, noted the growing devotion to St. Joseph, the increased blessings of this great saint, and the universal desire to see his veneration become more solemn. The signatory fathers, consequently, asked that he be proclaimed as the patron of the universal Church, which is the Body of Christ, and that his patronage would be a double of the first class.

The council had to break up prematurely because of the Franco-Prussian War of 1870-1871. But Pope Pius IX had heard the requests. As we noted above, on December 8, 1870, a decree of the Sacred Congregation of Rites declared St. Joseph to be the patron of the universal Church:

As almighty God appointed Joseph, son of the patriarch Jacob, over all the land of Egypt to save grain for the people, so when the fullness of time had come and he was about to send to earth his only-begotten Son, the Savior of the world, he chose another Joseph, of whom the first had been the type, and he made him the lord and chief of his household and possessions, the guardian of his choicest treasures.

Indeed, he had as his spouse the Immaculate Virgin Mary, of whom was born by the Holy Spirit, Jesus Christ our Lord, who deigned to be reputed in the sight of men as the son of Joseph and was subject to him whom countless kings and prophets had desired to see, Joseph not only saw but conversed with, and embraced in paternal affection, and kissed. He most diligently reared him whom the faithful were to receive as the bread that came down from heaven whereby they might obtain eternal life.

Because of this sublime dignity that God conferred on his most faithful servant, the Church has always most highly honored and praised blessed Joseph next to his spouse, the virgin mother of God, and has besought his intercession in times of trouble. And now therefore, when in these most troublesome times the Church is beset by enemies on every side, and is weighed down by calamities so heavy that ungodly men assert that the gates of hell have at length prevailed against her, the venerable prelates of the whole Catholic world have presented to the sovereign pontiff their own petitions and those of the faithful committed to their charge, praying that he would deign to constitute St. Joseph patron of the Church.

In this holy Vatican ecumenical council, they have renewed more ardently still their wish and this request, and it has now pleased our very holy father, Pope Pius IX, who has been moved by the deplorable situation that recent events have brought about, in order to entrust himself and all the faithful to the patriarch St. Joseph's most powerful patronage, has chosen to comply with the prelates' desire and has solemnly declared him patron of the Catholic Church. He has also ordered that his feast on March 19 be henceforth celebrated as a double of the first class; without any Octave, however, because of Lent.

The Church and St. Joseph

Pius XI wrote:

> We see and can only see the Blessed Virgin Mary, with her divine motherhood between Joseph and

God. The whole Church was near her, being contained like a fruitful seed in Christ's humanity and Blood. The entire Church was there—in the virginal motherhood of the most holy Virgin Mary, and mother of Jesus and the mother of all the faithful . . . Small in the eyes of men, but big in the eyes of the Spirit, the Church was near Joseph. He was the Holy Family's guardian and custodial father" (April 21, 1926).

Pope Leo XIII added that

the Holy Family, which Joseph ruled over with the authority of a father, contained within its limits the scarce-born Church. From the same fact that the most holy virgin is the mother of Jesus Christ is she the mother of all Christians whom she bore on Mount Calvary amid the supreme throes of the Redemption; Jesus Christ is, in a manner, the firstborn of Christians, who by the adoption and Redemption are his brothers.

And for such reasons the blessed patriarch looks upon the multitude of Christians who make up the Church as confided especially to his trust—this limitless family spread over the earth, over which, because he is the spouse of Mary and the father of Jesus Christ he holds, as it were, a paternal authority. It is, then, natural and worthy that as the blessed Joseph ministered to all the needs of the family at Nazareth and girt it about with his protection, he should now cover with the cloak of his heavenly patronage and defend the Church of Jesus Christ" (*Quamquam Pluries* 3).

And John Paul II:

Today we still have good reason to commend everyone to St. Joseph. It is my heartfelt wish that these
reflections on the person of St. Joseph will renew in
us the prayerful devotion that my predecessor called
for a century ago. Our prayers and the very person
of Joseph have renewed significance for the Church
in our day, in light of the third Christian millennium. The Second Vatican Council made all of us
sensitive once again to the "great things that God
has done," and to that "economy of salvation" of
which St. Joseph was a special minister.

Commending ourselves, then, to the protection
of him to whose custody God "entrusted his greatest
and most precious treasures" let us at the same time
learn from him how to be servants of the "economy
of salvation." May St. Joseph become for all of us an
exceptional teacher in the service of Christ's saving
mission, a mission that is the responsibility of each
and every member of the Church: husbands and
wives, parents, those who live by the work of their
hands or by any other kind of work, those called to
the contemplative life and those called to the apostolate.

The just man, who bore within himself the entire heritage of the Old Covenant, was also brought
into the "beginning" of the New and Eternal Covenant in Jesus Christ. May he show us the paths of
this saving covenant as we stand at the threshold of
the next millennium, in which there must be a con-
tinuation and further development of the "fullness
of time" that belongs to the ineffable mystery of the
Incarnation of the Word.

May St. Joseph obtain for the Church and for the
world, as well as for each of us, the blessing of the
Father, Son and Holy Spirit (*Redemptoris Custos* 28).

PART V

Joseph's Holiness

With the exception of the Virgin Mary, St. Joseph's holiness surpassed that of the other saints because of his very close relationship with the Messiah. The prophets announced the Messiah but neither saw nor heard him. The apostles and other saints served the Church, which is the mystical body of Christ. The martyrs testified to the Savior's coming. But Joseph, like Mary, was directly ordered to serve Christ.

Joseph's holiness was not clearly confirmed before the fifteenth century because the marriage of Mary and Joseph was considered exceptional and hard to offer as a model. Moreover, Joseph's having died before Jesus was a problem that a theologian like Eiximenis would explain on the basis of Joseph's closeness to Jesus and Mary.

Joseph's outstanding holiness can be understood, first of all, through the superabundance of graces and perfection that God put in his soul. "Sanctifying grace, which destines us to a supernatural union with God, is all the more abundant in a soul, such that this soul must be more intimately united to God in the supernatural order. So Joseph, both with respect to the Incarnate Word and the mother of God, received a very specific mission that had not been given to any other man."[74] Ubertino of Casale thought Joseph's holiness came from the graces that God had given him in accordance with his mission, whereas Olivi believed that it was an effect of Joseph's closeness to Jesus and Mary.

Joseph was the spouse of Mary and was reputed the Father of Jesus Christ. From these sources have sprung his dignity, his holiness, his glory. In truth, the dignity of the mother of God is so lofty that naught created can rank above it. But as Joseph has been united to the Blessed Virgin by the ties of marriage, it may not be doubted that he approached nearer than any to the eminent dignity by which the mother of God surpasses so nobly all created natures" (Leo XIII, *Quamquam Pluries*).

Joseph's outstanding holiness supersedes the holiness of every other saint—in relation to St. John the Baptist, first of all (see chapter 2). Here there is a difficulty that comes from Matthew 11:11, which states that "among those born of women no one has arisen greater than John the Baptist," which makes us think he was, in fact, the greatest saint of all. But Jesus was talking about John as the Old Covenant's greatest saint, whose last prophet he was.

Of course, St. Thomas Aquinas wrote about the apostles that "they received a more abundant grace than all the other saints, after Christ and the Virgin Mary" (Rom. 8:5). Yet Joseph's mission "was more advanced than that of the apostles. This required more graces, in accordance with St. Thomas's hypothesis. Suarez wrote that 'certain offices belong to the same order as sanctifying grace. The apostles had the highest-ranking order. So they needed more complimentary help than the others, especially regarding gifts that are freely given and wisdom. But there are other offices that verge on a hypostatic union order, which is more perfect in itself, as we clearly see in the Blessed Virgin Mary's divine motherhood. St. Joseph's ministry belonged to this order of offices.' Without wanting to draw any absolute conclusion, the great theologian 'estimated that it was neither rash nor ungodly, but, on the contrary, it was loving and credible to consider St. Joseph among the first of the saints to be filled with grace and bliss (in *Summa Theologica* III, q. 29, d. 8, s. 1)."[75]

In *La dévotion de St. Joseph* (*The Devotion of St. Joseph*), Pierre de Sainte-Marie assured that "St. Joseph was a universal saint. He was a saint who embraced all kinds of holiness, regardless of the order or condition. From the scepter to the staff, and from the cedars to the hyssop, nobody has been able to retreat from his shadow."

In a sermon he preached before the fathers at the Council of Constance, Gerson, the University of Paris's chancellor, maintained that Joseph was sanctified in his mother's womb. Several theologians went along with this, including Cornelius a Lapide, St. Alphonsus Maria Liguori, St. Francis de Sales, etc. This was also the case with Dom Marechaux, who believed that Joseph was "sanctified starting in his mother's womb by a grace that was exceptionally thoughtful, as was John the Baptist. It is reasonable to think that this latent infusion of light and grace entered into the harmony of high dignity to which God predestined him" (*Elevations About St. Joseph*). Dom Démaret included Joseph's sanctification in his mother's womb among the number of divine acts of thoughtfulness in his favor. Yet Scripture mentions this privilege of sanctification before birth only for John the Baptist and the prophet Jeremiah.

Joseph's holiness flowed, among other things, from his daily contact with Jesus and Mary. First of all with his spouse: "If the Holy Spirit called Joseph a righteous man, when he was chosen to be Mary's spouse, let us consider what an abundance of love and all virtues our saint must have taken away from the conversations with his holy spouse and her continual companionship. He saw a perfect model of all the virtues in her. If only one of Mary's words was enough to sanctify John the Baptist and fill Elizabeth with the Holy Spirit, we should think that Joseph's beautiful soul must have become really holy through the intimate relationship he had with Mary for at least twenty-five years, according to tradition!"[76]

Joseph was also sanctified thanks to Jesus' presence at his side: "How much more must St. Joseph's holiness have grown by the intimate relationship he shared with Jesus Christ, during all those years they lived together! The two disciples who went to Emmaus felt embraced by divine love during the few moments that they accompanied the Savior and heard him speak, as they later said: 'Were not our hearts burning within us while he was talking to us on the road?' (Luke 24:32). What must we think about the flames of charity that were developing in Joseph's heart during the thirty years he spent in the company of the Son of God, while listening to the words of eternal life coming out of his mouth and observing the perfect examples of humility, patience, and obedience he gave in being so prompt to help him in his work and serve him in everything at home? What a blaze of love all these dashes of fire must have stimulated in Joseph's heart—this heart that was untainted by all earthly affection!"[77]

St. John Eudes, who pointed out the close union that existed among the hearts of Jesus, Mary, and Joseph, believed that "after God, St. Joseph was his holy spouse's first love. He had the first place in her heart. For Mary was all for Joseph. As a wife is for her husband, Mary's heart belonged to Joseph. Not only did it belong to him, but if it is said that the first Christians only had one heart and soul [cf. Acts 1:14], all the more can we say that the Blessed Virgin Mary and her holy spouse only had one soul and heart via a sacred connection of love and charity. Thus, it is consistent that Joseph had only one heart with Mary. Whereupon we can say that since Mary had only one heart with Jesus, Joseph, consequently, had only one heart with Jesus and Mary. Just as with the adorable Trinity of the Father, Son, and Holy Spirit, there are three persons who have only one heart, in the same way, there were three hearts that were only one heart in the trinity of Jesus, Mary, and Joseph."

This holiness could only have grown over time. Joseph was free from all actual sin during his life.[6] He was destined to the lofty mission of being the guardian of the Holy Family. He was completely connected to the graces that God did not stop favoring him with. Grace continually grew in his soul, especially as he responded so well to it. In this way, he justified his name that, as we have said, means "God will add."

The Hypothesis of Joseph's Immaculate Conception

According to moral theology, *lust* means the tendency toward evil that exists in human nature as a result of the original sin committed by Adam and Eve, our first parents.

Despite his holiness, Joseph was inevitably marked by original sin. The dogmatic definition of the Immaculate Conception of Mary "does not say that this singular privilege is unique, but it hints at it. On the other hand, the affirmation of this uniqueness was explicitly stated in the encyclical *Fulgens corona* on September 8, 1953, when Pope Pius XII talked about 'this very specific privilege that was not ever granted to anyone else,' thus excluding the possibility,

---

6 This is a common opinion in the Catholic tradition, though not definitive Church teaching.

maintained by some, but without a real basis, of attributing it to St. Joseph as well."[78]

Nonetheless, Gerson did not hesitate to attribute privileges that were like Mary's to Joseph. He was sanctified "starting from his mother's womb," as John the Baptist had been. Joseph also benefited from the assumption of his body to heaven, although Gerson somewhat hesitatingly said so[79] (see chapter 1).

The idea of Joseph's immaculate conception emerged mainly in Spain. It was influenced by Fr. José Domingo Corbató (1862-1913). He thought that since Joseph belonged to the order of the hypostatic union, it was appropriate for him to be exempt from original sin. Father E. Cantera believed that Joseph's immaculate conception could be the object of private belief because it could not be proven. Father Andres de Ocerín de Jáuregui, O.F.M., based this immaculate conception on Joseph's predestination before our first parents' fall and on the holy patriarch's belonging to the hypostatic union, as well as on arguments from excellence, fittingness, and authority. Yet most contemporary theologians reject this notion about Joseph. Nonetheless, a stream of thought asserts that Pope Pius IX did not, strictly speaking, talk about Mary's unique privilege when he defined her immaculate conception with the papal bull *Ineffabilis Deus* in 1854. The tendency would rather be to accept it as a private opinion "because there are reasons to validate the existence of these privileges." Msgr. Luis y Pérez, the bishop of Oviedo, wrote this in 1925. The privileges in question were "Joseph's sanctification in his mother's womb and even his exemption from original sin" (R. Gauthier).

The Hypothesis of Joseph's Sinlessness

From his freedom from concupiscence, we can deduce Joseph's sinlessness: "As the husband of the immaculate Virgin Mary, St. Joseph was elevated to such a pure condition that we can say that his attraction to sin was extinguished. He lived without the shadow of sin here on earth via a privilege that resulted from his marriage to Mary and his being Jesus' father. He personally experienced for us that a soul that is continuously influenced by Mary's sanctity can become very holy. In short, Mary glorified Jesus through her exemption from sin. St. Joseph glorified Jesus and Mary through his impeccability and outstanding virtues."[80]

"We can devoutly believe that lust was so perfectly bound in St. Joseph, who was sanctified in his mother's womb, that this allowed him to avoid the least venial sin throughout his whole life—even an indeliberate one."[81]

Father Lépicier defended Joseph's impeccability by basing it on the perfect purity that Joseph's mission required.[82]

But we cannot prove that Joseph received this privilege. All that we can assert is that this patriarch was confirmed in grace as soon as he was married to Mary. As for the rest, "in order to avoid, in God's actual order, venial sins throughout one's life, even those that are somewhat deliberate, one needs help from God that is completely extraordinary. This has never been granted to a man who was conceived in sin, unless it was via a very special privilege whose existence is impossible to certify."[83] It would be more reasonable to believe that Joseph, "who was outstandingly formed in grace (which does not necessarily imply perpetual impeccability), did not stop increasing the supernatural treasure of graces that God had deposited into his soul from the time he reached the age of reason."[84]

Joseph's Virginity

Some apocryphal writings assert that Joseph was married before meeting Mary, and that he had children who were, according to them, called the Lord's "brothers and sisters" in the Gospels (see Chapter 1). The Eastern tradition has given a lot of credit to this statement precisely because it allows us to provide an easy answer to the issue of these brothers and sisters. This opinion is still found in Eastern liturgical books, especially Greek ones. Latin theologians have rejected it, with a few exceptions (St. Hilary of Poitiers, St. Gregory of Tours, and Ambrosiaster).

The thesis of Joseph's perpetual virginity was first expressed by St. Jerome.[85] It noted the general consent of the Latin Fathers and ecclesiastical writers, who thought it was true. The Fathers confirmed Joseph's complete chastity. They thought it was blasphemous or rash to think otherwise. "The type of marriage that the Holy Spirit guided Mary and Joseph toward is understandable only in the framework of a saving plan and great spirituality. The real-life fulfillment of the mystery of the Incarnation required a virginal birth that emphasized a divine lineage and, at the same time, a family that could guarantee the normal development of the child's personality. It is precisely for their contribution to the mystery of the Incarnation that Joseph and Mary received the grace to experience the charism of virginity and the gift of marriage together. The virginal communion of love of Mary and Joseph, although it was a completely specific case, was linked to the real-life fulfillment of the mystery of the Incarnation."[86]

A UNIQUE PLACE AMONG THE ANGELS AND SAINTS

In truth, the dignity of the mother of God is so lofty that naught created can rank above it. But as Joseph has been united to the Blessed Virgin by the ties of marriage, it may not be doubted that he approached nearer than any to the eminent dignity by which the mother of God surpasses so nobly all created natures. For marriage is the most intimate of all unions, which from its essence imparts a community of gifts between those that by it are joined together. Thus in giving Joseph the Blessed Virgin as spouse, God appointed him to be not only her life's companion, the witness of her maidenhood, the protector of her honor, but also, by virtue of the conjugal tie, a participator in her sublime dignity (Leo XIII, *Quamquam Curies* 3).

"The only example of Jesus Christ, who wanted to honor St. Joseph on earth, to the point of being under his authority, should stimulate an enthusiastic devotion to this great saint in all souls. The eternal Father designated him to take his place alongside his Son. Jesus always regarded him as his father. He gave him the respect and obedience a son should give his father for thirty years.[†] The gospel confirms that he was obedient to Mary and Joseph (cf. Luke 2:51). This means that, during all this time, the Redeemer's job was to obey them. As head of this small family, it was up to Joseph to be in charge, and up to Jesus to be submissive to him. He only took a step, acted, ate, and rested according

---

[†] This seems excessive, unless we place the start of our Lord's public life right after the holy patriarch's death.

to Joseph's orders.‡ He immediately obeyed him in everything Jean Gerson said that Jesus was often busy preparing the meal, washing dishes, collecting water, and sweeping the house. Jesus Christ's humble obedience elevated St. Joseph's dignity above that of all the other saints, except for the mother of God."[87]

Joseph had "a father's authority, care, and duties with regard to Jesus. Were any of the tasks of the best of fathers not gloriously carried out by this faithful and prudent servant that the Lord appointed to be in charge of his family? (cf. Matt. 24:45). . . . He was not only the friend of the spouse, like John the Baptist. He was his guardian and protector. He received him in his home, took him in his arms, and pressed him on his heart" (Duport).

"We must not doubt it," says Bernardine of Siena. "In heaven, Christ did not renounce the intimacy, respect, and very high dignity that he showed Joseph during his human life, like a son with regard to his father. Instead, he enriched and completed it."[88]

Theologians are constantly confirming Joseph's unique eminence compared to the angels and all the saints, including St. John the Baptist. "A triple eminence came out of him—the eminence of titles and qualities, virtues and merits, and intercession and mediation. This triple eminence ended with an eminence of holiness and glory."[89]

---

‡ But we can think Jesus was mentally free and, even more, loving enough to take the initiative and provide many services without Mary and Joseph's having to ask him for this.

Joseph and the Trinity

The Image of the Father

Jesus obeyed his Father in the Holy Spirit by conforming to everything Joseph did and asked him to do—this Joseph whom he called "father" on the earth. "The more the Son obeyed him, with this humility that characterized him, the more the humble Joseph was launched into a grandeur that was unique in the history of men. He was the Father's image."[90]

In this respect, Jean-Jacques Olier, S.S., a French priest and the founder of the Sulpicians, wrote that "the Father, having chosen this saint to demonstrate his image on earth, gave him a resemblance to his invisible and hidden nature. In my opinion, this saint is beyond the comprehension of the minds of men."

The Holy Spirit and Joseph

Joseph's annunciation created an inner transformation: "Joseph, through the gift of the Spirit, whom he welcomed in his spirit that was united to the spirit of the Virgin Mary, his wife, spiritually and supernaturally, became the father of the living and the father of Christ and of his body, which is the Church. It was not a simple moral patronage, but a real fatherhood, though it was not physical. His grace of fatherhood, which was completely unique, was to be indissolubly connected to his wife in order to share in her divine maternal love with regard to Christ and all those renewed by Christ's spirit" (Manteau-Bonamy[91]).

The love of Mary and Joseph suited the Spirit's mission: their conjugal love, in which their child was already "conceived" through the divine will that had impelled them to love each other in this way, suited the Holy Spirit's mission perfectly. It was in Mary's active desire for virginal motherhood, a wish that was still hidden from her, that the Holy Spirit arose in the Annunciation. He elevated this desire up to the source of the divine fruitfulness that defines him as original love. But, for Mary, this was not an isolated, individualist love, which the Spirit committed himself to in the gift of Christ that he gave her by giving of himself. She and Joseph had an authentic conjugal love.

Cooperator in the Incarnation of the Word

The hypostatic union is the "union of the divine and human nature, in the unity of Christ's personhood or hypostasis. Each nature preserves its own characteristics. The hypostatic union of Christ's human nature with the *Logos*, 'Divine Word,' was created during the conception of the Son of God in the Virgin Mary's womb. It was not interrupted when Christ died on the cross. Only his soul was separated from his body. The Lord's divinity was not separated from his humanity" (D. Le Tourneau).

If we look closely, we see that Joseph's mission surpassed the order of grace itself and was confined, through its term, to the *hypostatic order* that was established by the mystery of the Incarnation. But we must understand this well, by avoiding all exaggeration and understatement. Mary's unique mission, her divine maternity, ended in the hypostatic union—as did Joseph's hidden mission, in a sense. This doctrinal point was more explicitly confirmed by St. Bernard, by Bernardine of Siena, by the Dominican Isidore of Isolanis, by Suarez, and by many recent authors.

Bernard said this about Joseph: "He was the faithful and prudent servant that the Lord set up to support his mother, the foster father of his flesh, and the only faithful earthly collaborator of the great plan of the Incarnation."[92] Bernardine of Siena wrote: "When God chose someone, via grace, for a very lofty mission, he granted him all the gifts that were needed for this mission. This was outstandingly borne out for St. Joseph, our Lord Jesus Christ's foster father and Mary's husband."[93] Isidore of Isolanis also placed Joseph's vocation above that of the apostles. He noticed that their goal was to preach the gospel and enlighten and reconcile souls, but that Joseph's vocation was more immediately related to Christ himself because he was the husband of God's mother and the Savior's foster father and defender."[94]

Contemplation and Joseph

Since the "fatherly" love of Joseph the contemplative could have had an influence on the filial love of Jesus and, vice versa, the filial love of Jesus could have had an influence upon the fatherly love of Joseph, how can we manage, at length, to recognize this completely unique relationship? Those souls most sensitive to the impulse of divine love have rightly seen in Joseph a brilliant example of the interior life. Following St. Augustine's well known distinction between the love of the truth (*caritas veritatis*) and the practical demands of love (*necessitas caritatis*),[95] we can say that Joseph experienced both love of the truth—that pure contemplative love of the divine truth that radiated from the humanity of Christ—and the demands of love: that equally pure and selfless love required for his vocation to safeguard and develop the humanity of Jesus (John Paul II, *Redemptoris Custos* 27).

The specific grace of marriage, which required the Virgin Mary and Joseph to renounce sexual relations, "filled them with the clarity of the Holy Spirit. Their conversations, tenderness, and daily concern were aimed toward God. When their hearts overflowed toward each other, Mary felt that she should be loved only in accordance with God. She noticed a wake of tenderness coming out of Joseph's heart, passing near her, and going toward God. But this current was not going toward her. It was not the aim of its path. She preferred to believe that Joseph was not doing anything for her, but for God)."[96]

PRAYING TO ST. JOSEPH EVERY DAY

Fr. Patrignani recommended earmarking "every day of the week to one of St. Joseph's seven glorious privileges. The first day, honor him as Mary's husband. The second day, as Jesus' adoptive father. The third day, as the most pure virgin. The fourth day, as the eternal Father's vicar and partner. The fifth day, as the Holy Family's leader and protector. The sixth day, as the most fortunate of men in life and death. The seventh day, as the most elevated of all the saints in heaven."[97]

The Virtues of Joseph

The holy patriarch appeared to be a model of all the virtues, for "he was righteous, that is to say, embellished with the all the virtues and stainless.[98] Eusebius of Caesarea thought "we noticed a great freedom of thought, an incomparable modesty, and prudence that was on a par with his modesty. Above all, he was very devout, and his extraordinary beauty attracted people's attention."[99] Joseph was "the purest virgin man. He was also the one that was the most deeply humble and the most fervent in the love of God, the most contemplative, and the most attentive in serving of his wife, the Virgin Mary" (Ubertino of Casale).

St. Paul VI saw, in Joseph, the one who "introduced us to the Gospel of the Beatitudes. We see a docility in him and an exceptional promptness to obey. He completely submitted to the word that led him . . . to an extraordinary level of purity and sublimeness, which was higher than any human ambition. . . . Let us also approach the humble workshop's door in Nazareth, with the devotion of a child and like someone from the home. . . . There is no life that is not attacked by many dangers, temptations, weaknesses, and falls. Joseph, who was silent, good, gentle, and undefeated, teaches us what we must do."[100]

Let us briefly stop at one of the holy patriarch's innumerable virtues. We can deduct, first of all, from the evangelical accounts, that Joseph was very religious, honest, hardworking, obedient, gentle, and tenderly attached to Jesus and Mary. Matthew thought he was a "righteous man" (Matt. 1:19). His justice, even in a restricted sense, as a faithful observer of the Law, was accompanied by prudence, charity, gentleness, patience, faith, and obedience.

> He was not only a patriarch, but the bridegroom's guide at the head of all patriarchs. He was not only a confessor, but more than a confessor, for drawn up in this quality are the dignities of the bishops, the generosity of the martyrs and all the other saints. It is, therefore, right that he is compared to the palm tree, which is the king of trees. It has the attributes of virginity, humility, constancy, and bravery. These are three virtues that the glorious St. Joseph greatly excelled in. If we dared make any comparison, there are some who would maintain that he surpassed all the other saints in these three virtues.[101]

Eighteenth-century author Jean Richard put it this way:

Examine these prerogatives as much as you would like. Tell yourselves that, having been destined for the noblest ministry that ever existed, he gathered in himself what had been distributed to the other saints. He had the prophets' understanding to know the secrets of a divine Incarnation. He had the loving care of the patriarchs to nourish a man who was God. He had the faith of the apostles to discover the hidden greatness of a God in a man's outer humility. He had the zeal of the confessors and the strength of the martyrs to defend and save the life of a God at the risk of his own. Say all that, gentlemen. But I will answer you with a few words: *Joseph, her husband, was righteous.*[102]

We could have said:

Joseph is the only saint who practiced the virtues that were suitable for every condition [outside, obviously, of the Virgin Mary]. This is why he received the prerogative of being the only saint who can intercede for people from all walks of life.

In this sense, we can say that God gave him the right to bless all nations. *Benedictionem omnium gentium dedit illi* (Sir. 44:25).

Joseph belonged to a royal race, but he had to work from the work of his hands. So, the rich, the poor, nobles, and common people must all have recourse to him.

He was committed to a marriage. But he preserved the purest and most perfect virginity in this marriage. Thus, people who have made a vow of virginity and all those who are married must resort to him. [He continued to be a layman.] But, having had the honor of carrying Jesus Christ's very holy body between his hands and offering it to God, with the purest religious sentiments, he practiced the most noble and sublime of priesthoods. Therefore, laypeople, priests, and Church members must resort to him.

Yes, God gave him the power to bless all of the earth's tribes. There is no kingdom that does not have him as a protector. There is no family that does not have him as guardian. There is no Christian who does not have him as an advocate. His name, which is united to that of Jesus and Mary, is the confidence, consolation, honey, and sweetness of all Christian lips."[103]

In his sermon "*Quaesivit sibi Deus virum iuxta cor suum*," Bossuet returned to the hidden and interior virtues, the ones in which "the public has no share in and where everything occurs between God and man. They are the ones that, not only are not followed, but are not even heard. . . . The whole mystery of true virtue is in this secret." These three hidden virtues of the fair Joseph are simplicity, detachment, and a love for the hidden life. Joseph appears as the model for all human conditions.

Joseph's Faith

As soon as the angel announced to him that the child that Mary was waiting for came from God, he submissively bowed down and did not look for the reasons for this miracle. He unhesitatingly and, without delay, believed it. As soon as he woke up, he did what the angel had commanded him to do (Matt. 1:21). Bossuet explained that in this way, he surpassed Abraham's faith (see chapter 2), for Abraham believed only in a sterile woman giving birth, whereas Joseph believed in a virgin giving birth. Joseph did not witness Jesus' miracles. He knew only about human nature's weaknesses. He saw Jesus as small and frail and dependent on his parents in all his needs. He worked by his side as a simple craftsman, etc. So much humiliation, weakness, powerlessness, infirmity, and so many needs did not shake his faith for an instant—a faith that was, all that being said, exceptionally firm, expansive, and enlightened.

One can say that *what Joseph did* united him in an altogether special way to Mary's faith. He accepted as a truth coming from God *the very thing that she had already accepted* at the Annunciation. The Council taught: "'The obedience of faith' must be given to God, as he reveals himself. Man freely commits himself entirely to God through this faithful obedience. He 'fully submits his intellect and will to God who reveals himself,' and willingly assents to the revelation that he gives." This statement, which touches on the very essence of faith, *is perfectly applicable to Joseph of Nazareth.*

Therefore, he became the unique guardian of the mystery "hidden for ages in God" (see Eph. 3:9) (*Redemptoris Custos* 4, 5).

On Christmas night, Joseph, while taking the newborn baby in his arms, did not hesitate to recognize that he was the Son of God. "He recognized the uncreated wisdom of this Word that the Father pronounced in an eternal today in this newborn baby. . . . His faith broke through the appearance and penetrated into the divine. . . . During his adoration, he became aware of the ministry that he was going to practice. God entrusted his Son to him to take care of him" (M. Gasnier[104]).

Joseph's Hope

This virtue "cautioned him against two diametrically opposed extremes—presumption and despair. Presumption could have tempted him because of the grace that heaven had filled him with. Despair could have brought him down in view of the tribulations that kept afflicting him. But his faith in God prevented him from becoming spineless, which could have harmed him. It allowed him, at the same time, to glimpse God's promptness, which was never going to abandon him."[105]

Perhaps Joseph was not any more hopeful than when he accepted the mission of taking care of Jesus and Mary, his spouse. She was the foundation of the confidence and serenity that Joseph demonstrated throughout his life, especially when the angel asked him to take the child and his mother and flee into Egypt, in an unknown land where they would be unknown. He promptly and simply acted because he was assured that God would watch over him and the precious dual guardianship entrusted to him.

Joseph's Charity

First of all, Joseph loved God with his whole heart, mind, and strength. He loved his own soul and wanted to make it always more closely resemble its divine author. Finally, he loved his own body, which he regarded as the instrument of the good works that he accomplished. With respect to the love of God and his neighbor, "we must notice how intensely this love grew in Joseph because these two loves were concentrated in the same person. Jesus was both God and man. Thus, by loving Jesus, he, with one act, loved Mary, his Creator, his Son, and his Savior. These three loves came together to form a cluster of incomparable warmth and splendor."[106]

The love he had for Mary and Jesus could not be an obstacle to God's love for him. In fact:

> Natural love and divine love, the love of his son and the love of his God, had only one and the same object. In him, nature and grace, far from splitting his affections, on the contrary, brought them together

and kindled them more. He was zealously devoted and a happy father, who could love his son right up to the point of loving him too much. He could give everything to his son without taking away anything from his God, could join and harmonize the fires of heaven and earth! Oh father, who is happy once again, in whom the foolhardiness of love did not have to be corrected, as it needed to be in others".[107]

Joseph's Obedience

This virtue shines like the others in the holy patriarch.

> *Exurgens autem Ioseph a somno.* . . . Having awoken from sleep, Joseph did as the angel of the Lord commanded him. He took Mary as his wife (Matt. 1:24). Joseph's obedience was:
>
> 1) *Commanded.* This was, first of all, about abandoning vices to acquire virtues. This is why it says *exurgens a somno.*
>
> 2) *Prompt.* He immediately did what love asked him to do. Delaying is, in a way, preferring our will to the Lord's. There will perhaps be no more time to do what has been commanded for us to do when we finally want to obey.
>
> 3) *Perfect.* He did what the angel asked him to do in the way that was indicated to him by complying with what the angel had called for. He did this, not only to accomplish it, but also for other circumstances of time, place, and attitude.
>
> 4) *Prudent.* He obeyed the angel—the one he had to obey.[108]

Or, as Alphonsus put it:

> Joseph was resigned to the will of the eternal Father who wanted his Son, from his childhood, to suffer to expiate men's sins. But his tender and loving heart could not help but feel a keen sense of sorrow while listening to Jesus cry because of the cold and other inconveniences that he experienced.[109]

AN EXAMPLE OF OBEDIENCE

Regarding the flight into Egypt, St. John Chrysostom declared:

> Therefore, the angel appeared and spoke, not to Mary, but to Joseph: *Get up. Take the child and his mother.* He did not say as before: *Take your spouse,* but take the mother of Jesus. The birth had taken place. There was no more suspicion. The husband's faith was firm. The angel could openly talk to him. This is why he clearly said to Joseph: *Take the child and his mother, and flee to Egypt.* He gave him the reason: *For Herod is about to search for the child in order to kill him.*
>
> Joseph was not scandalized by this unexpected order and said nothing to the angel. What an enigma! Once, you were saying that this child would save his people, and now he cannot save himself. We are forced to flee and emigrate a long way away. The events are contrary to your promise. He did not even think about expressing himself in this way. He silently obeyed. He did not think more about the time of the return, although the angel had

very vaguely spoken about it. *Remain there until I tell you.* He zealously obeyed without further delay, and bravely confronted all of the trip's hazards.

God, in his goodness, mixed joy and sadness in this meeting. He did not allow them to be continually endangered or secure. Good and evil alternate in the lives of the righteous. This was Joseph's fate. First of all, he saw that his betrothed was pregnant—trouble, chagrin, born of a terrible suspicion. Then, the angel came right away, dispersed the suspicion, and freed him from his fears. Afterwards, the birth occurred, along with the joy that it brought. This was a temporary joy that the fear of danger soon drove away. The city rioted, and the enraged king tried to kill the child.

This disruption was immediately tempered by joy, which was provoked by the star and the adoration of the Magi. Then there were other worries. Herod wanted to kill the child, and the angel urged Joseph to flee and go into exile—to act according to the human condition because the time to perform miracles had not yet come.

Joseph's Beauty

The beauty that heaven had gifted him with was admirable in that it really approached the beauty of Jesus, who is the miracle of beauty. God's goodness used the resemblance between Jesus and Joseph, via their facial features, their bearing and outward good grace and symmetry, and other excellent arrangements of their bodies, to let the Jews continue to claim that Jesus of Nazareth was really Joseph's son.[110]

David's beauty was passed on to all his descendants.

The Scripture notes this—even when his sons used this dangerous beauty in a criminal way. . . .
 The son of David, who was betrothed to the most beautiful of women, was chosen by God to become the virginal father of the most beautiful of children. Who could doubt that Joseph would have received this heritage of his race? He had to be beautifully youthful, strong, and candid" (Buzy[111]).

Joseph's Strength of Soul

We see that the holy patriarch was constantly sustained by the virtue of strength. He patiently bore the different trials that he was subject to—the uncertainly about his beloved spouse's moral state; the fear of death—regarding Jesus as well as Mary and himself, following Herod's persecution; and the worry inflicted by the child left in Jerusalem. The litanies of St. Joseph invoke him in this way: *Joseph fortissime, ora pro nobis.*

Joseph's Humility

This virtue, so essential, brightly shone in Joseph. He was often led to act humbly.

He proved this by perfectly conforming to the divine will, without a whisper, he whose ancestors had once ruled over Israel—his family's decline and the obscure life of a simple day laborer. He showed it by joyfully withdrawing into a hidden and poor existence. He showed it by remaining silent before the choice that God had made for him to cooperate in the accomplishment of his merciful plans. Above all, he showed it by hiding, with jealous care, the great graces that he had received and the glorious mission that he had been honored with.[112]

Humility leads to the detachment from one's passions.

> St. John Chrysostom was surely right to admire Joseph's philosophy here. Joseph was, he said, a great philosopher who was perfectly detached from his passions because we see him overcome the most tyrannical one. A man who is capable of getting sober advice, and having taken it so wisely, postpones its implementation, and sleeps within these thoughts is really in charge of his actions. If his soul had not been calm, believe that the lights from on high would not have descended right away. It is, therefore, unquestionable, my brothers, that he was very detached from his passions—whether the most enticing gentle ones or the fiercest violent ones, particularly love and jealousy.[113]

At the same time, this humility led Joseph to die to himself:

> Buried with Jesus Christ and . . . Mary, he did not mind this death, which made him live with the Savior. On the contrary, he did not fear anything even as the age's noise and life came to disturb or interrupt this hidden interior rest. An admirable mystery: Joseph had something that attracted the eyes of the whole world, which did not know him. He possessed a God-Man and did not say a word about it. He witnessed such a great mystery and secretly savored it without divulging it.[114]

As Fr. Frederick Faber, a nineteenth-century priest and convert from Anglicanism, put it:

> The foundation, therefore, of Joseph's devotion was, as with Mary, his humility. Its eye was always on its

own unworthiness. It was a humility that forever seemed surprised at its own gifts, and yet so tranquil that there was nothing in it either of the precipitation or the ungracefulness of a surprise. He was unselfishness itself, the very personification of it. . . .

With the deepest reverence he hid himself in the constant thought of the dignity of his office, in the profoundest self-abjection. . . . St. Joseph's humility was fed all through life by having to command Jesus, by being the superior of his God.[115]

His humility was accompanied by a spirit of service. "Joseph always continued to be the servant of Jesus and Mary— Jesus' servant *in* Mary and Mary's servant *for* Jesus. Such was the devotion he had for them, that is to say, the unlimited devotion with which he served them, and the veneration he unceasingly gave them" (Fr. Joseph de Sainte-Marie[116]).

The presence of such humility in Joseph is the reason why he deserves to be highly glorified and honored.

Joseph's Purity

St. Augustine developed the argument of Joseph's being Jesus' father and his chastity in considerable detail:

Just as the marriage of [Mary] and Joseph was real, and not covetous, why would the son that Mary's virginity conceived not have been received by the chaste Joseph? He was a chaste husband, just as she was a chaste wife. Why would he not be a father, virgin as he was, just as Mary deserved to be a mother, without ceasing to be a virgin? Thus, the one who claims that Joseph should not be called a father because he did not create a son is looking for the satisfaction of lust and not the tenderness of affection. Joseph accomplished much more perfectly in his heart what others desire to accomplish in a sexual way. . . . Why was he a father? He was in a sense that was all the more true as it was in virtue of a greater chastity. We undoubtedly thought Joseph was the father of our Lord Jesus Christ in a completely different way, that is to say, as are biological fathers, who conceive not merely through spiritual affection. This is why St. Luke said: "Son (as was thought) of Joseph." The Lord was not Joseph's son according to nature, although we thought he was. Nonetheless, thanks to Joseph's devotion and charity, the Virgin Mary gave birth to a son, who was, at the same time, the Son of God.[117]

St. Leonard of Port Maurice commented on the emotion that Mary felt when the angel Gabriel came. "What! Mary troubled herself before a resident of heaven. Who would be sufficiently happy not to scare off such modesty? It would be St. Joseph." By taking Joseph as her husband, Mary "showed that she had an even greater confidence, if that is possible, in the discretion and respect of St. Joseph than in the discretion and respect of an angel who, to manifest himself to her, had to put on a human form."

Joseph's Fidelity

Bossuet reminds us that

"when Jesus entered somewhere, he entered there with his cross, he carried it there with all its thorns, and he shared with it all those he loved." After having mentioned Jesus' birth conditions and the flight into Egypt, he asked: "Was it sufficient to test his fidelity? Christians, do not believe it. Here is another strange trial. If few men tormented him, Jesus became his persecutor. He skillfully escaped from his hands. He became inattentive and was lost for three days. . . . See, faithful ones, by what sufferings Jesus proves people's faith, and how much he wants to be with only those who suffer.[118]

Joseph's Prudence

The prudence of Saint Joseph is part of our Catholic faith. It is especially shown in his remarkable practice of silence. Of course, Joseph talked. Yet the Gospels do not record a single word he spoke, no doubt to teach us that if we wish to practice the virtue of prudence, we must look to our practice of silence. . . .

St. Joseph teaches us that prudence is correct knowledge about things to be done or, more broadly, the knowledge of things that ought to be done and of things that should be avoided.[119]

More than once, Joseph had to practice this virtue in difficult circumstances—when he decided to dismiss his wife in secret in view of her unexpected pregnancy, when they returned from the exile in Egypt, and in the choice of where to live upon recovering Jesus in the temple.

Joseph's Patience

To be patient "is to bear, without complaining or being discouraged, the evils that press upon us, however long they may be." According to St. Thomas, it is also reacting victoriously against the sadness caused by the actual pressure of evil and, as a result, maintaining a holy joy in one's heart. According to St. Alphonsus Liguori,

How patient St. Joseph was, from this dual perspective! . . . He constantly considered taking on himself all pain and anguish and not allow any of it go to Mary and Jesus. His patience was a shield that received and blunted the enemies' strokes. His vocation and happiness consisted of sacrificing himself every day to benefit Jesus and Mary.

Joseph's Poverty

Pope Pius XII wrote:

> Before the king of heaven, who trembled in the straw and who still had no language, like every man who comes into this world, but crying: *et primam vocem similem omnibus emisi plorans*, "my first sound was a cry" (Wis. 7:3), Mary and Joseph saw, in an inner light that illuminated the very aspect of material realities, that the most blessed child of God is not necessarily the one who is born into riches and well-being.[120]
>
> Even if he had few material goods, Joseph, nevertheless, was happy with his lot. We never see him try to take advantage of his title as a descendant of David. It was enough for him to be what God wanted him to be. . . . Yet his poverty did not take anything away from his nobility. . . . It made him a privileged and an extremely joyful prince. . . . He was very much this righteous man that his ancestor had sung about, accompanied by his harp (M. Gasnier).

On Joseph's detachment:

> Christians, let us learn, through the example of St. Joseph, to conquer these sweets that charm us and this loss of our temper. See how detached he is from his passions because he could overcome, without resisting, the most flattering sweets and the fiercest violence. I mean love and jealousy. . . .

He was [Chrysostom said] a great philosopher, who was perfectly detached from his passions since we see him overcome the most tyrannical of all of them. . . . He kept going, nonetheless, without worrying and always wandering, only because he was with Jesus Christ. He was all too happy to possess him at this price. He considered himself all too rich. Every day, he tried once again to empty his heart, so that God would stretch out his possessions and expand his reign there. He was abundant because he had nothing. He possessed everything because he was lacking everything. He was happy, calm, and confident because he came across not rest, nor home, nor consistency. This was the last result of Joseph's detachment, and the one that we must more reflectively notice. For our most common vice and the one that is the most opposed to Christianity is an unfortunate tendency to set up shop on earth.[121]

Joseph's Simplicity

Joseph "abandoned himself to God in a simple way and carried out all that he ordered him to do without questioning it. In effect, obedience is too curious when it searches out the reasons for the command. . . . But Joseph's obedience came from the fact that he believed in simplicity, and his mind did not wobble between reason and faith. It very intentionally followed the lights that came from above."[122]

Joseph's Knowledge

Acquired knowledge, in the holy patriarch, was what it is in us—namely, the result of the activity of our understanding and the instruction that our parents and teachers give us.

Joseph was given innate knowledge, which was communicated directly to his soul on various occasions. This happened when the angel invited him to keep Mary as his wife, despite her obvious pregnancy, and when he fled into Egypt to return to Israel, to retreat to Galilee. Thus also was he invited to be more fully initiated into the knowledge of heavenly mysteries that dealt with the Incarnation of the Word, in which he played such a large part.

We have to exclude blessed knowledge, which is specific to the elect. But, Cdl. Lépicier wondered, "can we believe that, at least, at certain times of his life, St. Joseph temporarily saw the divine essence through a privilege that was like, according to St. Thomas, the one that was granted to Moses and St. Paul?" He responded with "negative, because of the silence of Scripture and because such a privilege was not required by his mission, which was very different from the mission of Moses and St. Paul."

Work and Joseph

Jesus came to his hometown and began to teach the people in their synagogue, in such a way that they were astounded and said, "Where did this man get this wisdom and these deeds of power? Is not this the carpenter's son?" (Matt. 13:54-55). This passage refers to Joseph's professional activity. Tradition recalls that he was a carpenter. This word, from the Greek, *tekton*, includes several technical skills, like being a craftsman, for example. Fr. Schwelm offered very credible specifications about what was made in the Nazareth workshop: "We can imagine that the orders conformed to a Jewish carpenter's known works—beams to be squared off on terraces that were on top of houses, yokes and arrows for hitching and prodding for farmers, beds, trunks, bread bins, kneading machines for housewives, notebook cases for scribes, storekeepers, and rabbis. The Mishna revealed that these various jobs were performed by carpenters."[123]

The fact that the Jews referred specifically to the work of Joseph, who was considered a righteous man, indicates that his qualities as a worker were recognized and appreciated. Joseph was an honest worker who strove to live according to his means—what he got out of his work. In this way, he sanctified his work. John Paul II said that "at the workbench where he plied his trade together with Jesus, Joseph brought human work closer to the mystery of the redemption" (*Redemptoris Custos* 22).

God also wanted Joseph's work to be used for Jesus Christ's human growth by stipulating that his Son's mission would be rooted in family life. As a result, Joseph's work contributed to the Redeemer's mission. Because he put his professional qualities in the service of the divine plan, Joseph showed us that work is a means of sanctification. "We cannot imagine that Joseph was not a good worker and that he was not known as much for his skill and competence as for his honesty and uprightness. People in Nazareth and the whole region knew that by speaking to him, they did not risk being ripped off. He was in the habit of delivering conscientious work" (Gasnier[124]).

Pierre d'Ailly[125] rightly saw Joseph as a worker. Asking himself how Jesus "received his food and the things that were needed for his human life," he responded: "Undoubtedly, through Joseph's manual work. We believe that Mary and Joseph were poor people, but it was never written that they ever begged. We also conclude that Joseph sustained his life with the work of his hands, while meditating in this way on this beatitude that was promised by his father David: 'You will then feed yourself from the work of your hands and will be happy and prosperous.'. . . Joseph could eat his bread on the earth through work—the one who lives in heaven without any need."[126]

> St. Joseph did not look for an opportunity to assert himself in his work, although because of his dedication to a life of work, he developed a mature and

well-defined personality. By working, the patriarch was aware of accomplishing God's will. He thought of his family—of Jesus and Mary—and he was conscious of the welfare of all the residents in the village of Nazareth. . . . Thanks to meticulous work, Joseph, undoubtedly, helped a lot of people get out of trouble. The goal of his professional work was to serve the other families in the village and make life pleasant for them. He smiled, spoke kindly, and made comments. This was done as if by chance. But it restored faith and joy to the ones who were on the verge of losing them.[127]

St. Joseph's Prayer

Saint Joseph stands before you as a man of faith and prayer. The liturgy applies to him the word of God in Psalm 89: "He shall say of me, 'You are my father, my God, the rock, my Savior'" (v. 27). O yes: how many times in the course of long days of work would Joseph have raised his mind to God to invoke him, to offer him his toil, to implore light, help, comfort. How many times! Well then, this man, who with his whole life seemed to cry out to God: "You are my father," receives this most special grace: the Son of God on earth treats him as his father.

Joseph invokes God with all the ardor of his soul as a believer: "my Father," and Jesus, who worked at his side with the tools of a carpenter, addressed him calling him "father." St. Joseph stands before you as a man of faith and prayer. The liturgy applies to him the word of God in Psalm 89: "He shall say of me 'You are my father, my God, the rock, my Savior'" (v. 26). Oh yes, how many times in the course of long days of work, did Joseph lift his thought to

God to invoke him, to offer him his toil, to implore light, help, comfort. Oh yes: how many times in the course of long days of work would Joseph have raised his mind to God to invoke him, to offer him his toil, to implore light, help, comfort. How many times! Well then, this man, who with his whole life seemed to cry out to God: "You are my father," receives this most special grace: the Son of God on earth treats him as his father. Joseph invokes God with all the ardor of his soul as a believer: "my Father," and Jesus, who worked at his side with the tools of a carpenter, addressed him calling him "father."[128]

The interior acts of the virtue of religion—to pray and adore God—were radiant in Joseph's life. By faithfully observing the Mosaic law, he performed the external acts, often spent time in the synagogue, and went to Jerusalem on a pilgrimage at the prescribed times.

> St. Augustine compared the other saints to stars, but St. Joseph to the sun. Father Suarez thought it was very reasonable to think that St. Joseph, after Mary, outdid all the other saints in merit and glory. Hence, the venerable Bernardino de Bustis concluded that, in heaven, St. Joseph, in a way, commands Jesus and Mary when he wants to get some grace for his servants.[129]

The song of the *Magnificat* that the Virgin Mary chanted in her cousin Elizabeth's home was from the Lord's poor people (see chapter 2). It also expresses the spirituality of Joseph, who came from this environment. In this chant, God fills the humble who have trusted him. The *Magnificat* expresses the spiritual environment in which Jesus grew—this life in Nazareth where three poor and honest people, who were faithful to God, worked and dwelled in silence and love. Nothing distinguished them in the eyes of the world. . . . Joseph and Mary provided the conditions to enable the man of the Beatitudes to grow. One day, he would express them in all their power. But it is not excessive to think that it was in this environment of growth that Jesus could start to experience them, to see them being experienced, and to learn them. . . . The *Magnificat* leads to the Beatitudes. The spirituality of Yahweh's poor people is brought to fruition in them (Pierre Robert[130]).

Master of the Interior Life

Here is a qualifier that St. Josémaria gave to St. Joseph:

St. Joseph, our most chaste and pure Father and Lord, who deserved to carry the child Jesus in your arms, and to wash and kiss him, teach us to become intimate with our God, and to be pure and worthy of being other Christs. Teach us to act like Christ—to make our paths divine (whether they are obscure or luminous)—and to teach men to do the same thing by telling them that they can be extraordinarily efficient on the earth.[131]

We easily understand that Joseph can be offered to us as a model. St. Bonaventure was the first of the great doctors of the Church to do this. He commented on the verse from Matthew (2:14) in a sermon around 1270: "got up, took the child and his mother." He said:

In these words of the Gospel, we are given a short and useful method of salvation that is the following: let the one who wants to save himself devotedly accept and receive the newborn Christ and his mother, in order to imitate and venerate them. In this way, he will reach the land of Israel, to know God's shining and eternal vision. Christ must be devotedly accepted and welcomed by everyone, in order to be venerated, following the example of Joseph, who accepted him in this way. . . . Likewise, the divine child's mother must be accepted in order to venerate her and have her before us, following the example of blessed Joseph. She is the accomplished model of evangelical humanity, of the Church's devotion, of all Christian devotion, and of the perfect love of these two subjects: God and neighbor.

Franciscans were the first ones to suggest Joseph as a model, foremost for the clergy. Speaking of the reasons for the marriage of Joseph and Mary, Peter John Olivi[132] presented the last in these terms:

Ninthly, to announce a greater mystery, that is to say, Christ, who was spiritually born from this spiritual marriage, in the hearts of the faithful and in the Church of God. Joseph referred to God the Father, or Christ, as the spouse of the Church, or the prelates who are the spouses of the Church. They, like Mary, must have a virgin faith and be innocent, according to the apostle in 2 Corinthians 11:2: "I promised you in marriage to one husband, to present you as a chaste virgin to Christ." Evangelical religion which, like Mary, understands the

evangelical word through Christ's Spirit, also represents the Roman pontiffs, who were given to him
as a guardian for a certain time. This occurred up
to the time when the little child, who was the heir
and Lord of all, freed himself from the weight of
guardians and trustees (Gal. 4:1-2).

In this text, we note "the critique of the ecclesial institution, if only through the two scriptural quotations which,
if we quote them entirely, allude to the Church's decadence
and the eschatological freedom from the secular clergy's
guardianship. In this perspective, Joseph is a model for all
clerics—especially the highest-ranking ones, starting with
the pope."[133]

PART VI

St. Joseph's
Apparitions
and
Miracles

We report here, by way of example, some of the holy patriarch's apparitions and miracles attributed to his intercession.

The Apparitions

Gaspard Ricard d'Estienne

St. Joseph's primary apparition in France occurred in Cotignac, in the department of Var. It followed one of the Virgin Mary's apparitions, occurring a century and a half later.

Indeed, on August 10, 1519, the Virgin Mary, who was carrying the child Jesus on one arm, and was surrounded by St. Bernard, St. Catherine the Martyr, and St. Michael, appeared to a butcher named Jean de la Baume in Cotignac. She charged him with a mission: "Go tell the clergy and the consuls of Cotignac to build me a church here named Our Lady of Graces, and have people proceed to receive the gifts that I want to leave there." The sanctuary was completed in 1521.

On November 3, 1637, at Notre-Dame-des-Victoires, in Paris, Denys Antheaume, whose religious name was Fiacre of St. Marguerite (1600-1684), a lay brother of the Augustinian monastery, called on the Virgin Mary for the birth of an heir to the French throne. She appeared to him four times. While the king and queen were late in having a child, Mary presented a child to the brother, saying: "He is not my son, but the child that God wants to give France." She asked the queen for three pilgrimages—one to Notre-Dame-de-Paris, the second one to Our Lady of Grace, in Provence, and the third to Our Lady of Victory, in Paris. Br. Fiacre described the Provence sanctuary, which he had never seen, by which everyone believed in his vision. Louis XIV, whose first name was Dieudonné, was born the following year. On February 21, 1660, Louis XIV, then twenty-two years old, came to Cotignac to thank Our Lady of Grace for his birth.

THE ORIGIN OF THE FIACRES

Once the reputation of Fiacre's holiness had spread, carriage coachmen took on the habit of placing his effigy on their vehicles, which ended up being called *fiacres*.

On June 7, 1660, while Louis XIV went to the Spanish border to welcome the princess Marie-Thérèse, the new queen of France, Joseph appeared to a thirsty shepherd named Gaspard Ricard d'Estienne. He pointed out a huge rock to him under which he would find a spring: "I am Joseph. Lift this rock, and you will drink." Looking up and down at the rock, Gaspard said: "I cannot. It is much too heavy." But the visitor repeated his command. So the shepherd managed to lift the rock by himself. (Later, eight were needed to make it budge.) Water began to flow on the spot. Gaspard recognized: "It was St. Joseph. He gave me the power."

Cotignac's residents were skeptical at first. They went on the premises and noticed that the water was now flowing abundantly. Soon, healings occurred, which attracted crowds to the Bessillon woods. A devotion to Joseph rapidly spread beyond Provence. As of August 9, 1660, the commune's consuls had a chapel built in honor of Joseph.

Communication with the sanctuary of Our Lady of Grace was carried out via the path of the crests, in the midst of which was an oratory dedicated to the child Jesus. In an order, dated January 31, 1661, the bishop of Fréjus, Msgr. Joseph Zongo Ondedei, officially recognized Joseph's apparitions in Cotignac and approved the site's veneration. He declared, in front of the assembly of the French clergy, that he "could not better entrust the administration of the husband's chapel than to those who were doing so well with the wife's chapel"—namely, the oratorians. That same year and following these marvelous events, King Louis XIV consecrated France to Joseph, the head of the Holy Family. On this occasion, Bossuet expressed himself with these words: "Joseph deserved the greatest honors because he was never affected by honor. The Church has nothing more illustrious because it has nothing more hidden."

Our Lady of Grace was destroyed during the Revolution and rebuilt in 1810. The current pilgrimage site's pastoral ministry was entrusted to the Brothers of St. John. The St. Joseph chapel was restored in 1978 by a community of Benedictine sisters. This is their conventual chapel. It is a well-frequented pilgrimage site, established as a minor basilica in 2005.

Joseph's statue is three kilometers from the Marian sanctuary, at the top of the Bessillon hill. In this way, it overlooks the Benedictine monastery and the fountain in which water miraculously spurted in the seventeenth century.

Jeanne des Anges (1602–65)

Jeanne de Belcier [her given name] was an Ursuline nun in Lyon. She always had Joseph's life on her mind, to meditate on its features and imitate it. Thanks to him, she was delivered from demons that obsessed her and was healed of a deadly disease that led her to death's door. One day, the saint appeared to her, more beautiful than the sun, and urged her to bear her pain consistently and to trust God completely. He asked her to go to Holy Communion nine times in his honor on the days of the week that corresponded to the one on which his feast fell.

Sister Mary Catherine of Saint Augustine (1632–68)

She was an Augustinian French hospital nun, born in Long-pré, who served in Mercy Hospital in Quebec (Canada). She added *Joseph* to her name, thenceforth called *Marie-Joséphine*. She had a vision on the Feast of the Ascension of our Lord. While the procession of the blessed rose to heaven, she distinguished Joseph preceding them all. He was directing their walk and was the one who was the closest to the eternal gates. Once Jesus was seated at the right hand of the Father, she heard Joseph speaking to the eternal Father: "Here is the talent that you entrusted to me on earth. I give it back to you, not only doubled but a hundredfold—as many times as there are souls in this crowd whose price he paid." The eternal Father responded: "Faithful servant, as you were the head of my [holy] family on earth, I want your power to be still the same in heaven, and for you to keep the title, not of a servant, but of Lord." On April 9, 1663, St. Joseph had already appeared to her in the company of Jean de Brébeuf, who often visited the nun and helped her pray.

Stobienia

Around 1670, a man named Stobienia, who was seriously ill with no hope of a cure, in Kalisz, Poland, prayed to God to let him die. He addressed himself to Joseph, the patron of a happy death. The following night, an elderly man, in whom he recognized the saint, came to his home. He said to him: "You will be healed when you have this family painting painted with the inscription: 'Go to Joseph' [see chapter 2]. You will offer it to the collegiate church in Kalisz." Once he was done, Stobienia kissed him, and he was healed. He had the painting placed in the collegiate church. It was honored in 1786. A sanctuary was then built to St. Joseph of Kalisz. On June 4, 1997, Pope John Paul II went there and gave a long homily that showed that "Joseph of Nazareth, who saved Jesus from Herod's cruelty, was now getting up in front of us as a spokesman for the defense of human life from the moment of conception to natural death."

Giacomo Moser, from the Montagnaga di Pine

In the province of Trentino (Italy), he had the habit of going to the sanctuary of Our Lady of Caravaggio. He brought back an image of this Virgin Mary, which he had placed in the church in the early eighteenth century. The Virgin Mary appeared there several times. The third time was on September 8, 1729. She was carrying the Christ child, wounded and losing blood, in her arms and accompanied by Ss. Joachim, Anne, and Joseph. Mary explained that her son's wounds were due to sins and urged Giacomo to pray much for the conversion of sinners.

And Still Others . . .

Benoîte Rencurel, the seer of Our Lady of Laus (1647-1718), also saw Joseph. On August 21, 1879, the Lamb of God's apparition in Knock, Ireland, was accompanied by Mary and a young Joseph, as well as St. John, who was holding the Gospel open.

On an unspecified date, someone pointed out the apparition of a "very dignified worker with a plane on his shoulder and a saw in his hand" to a poor woman who was coming back from the market in Plumelin, near Locminé, in Morbihan. Having invited her to ask Joseph for "the grace to live and die well," the man predicted to her that "great things will be done here. Many will come here from far away to live together." In the middle of the nineteenth century, the Congregation of the Daughters of Jesus and St. Joseph of Locmaria emerged on the site of this apparition.

During the Virgin Mary's last apparition in Fátima (Portugal), on October 13, 1917, the seers saw the sun's rotation and fall, as everyone did, in a succession of brief and swift images. Our Lady was dressed in white. Joseph and the child Jesus were dressed in scarlet red. Francisco and Jacinta said that "the child was in St. Joseph's arms. He was a very small child who was about a year old. He was no taller than the little Déolinda de José das Neves [a baby from their village]. He was dressed, like St. Joseph, in light red." After becoming a nun in Nevers, Sr. Lucia explained that Joseph was carrying the child Jesus and that "both of them seemed to bless the world with gestures that they were making with their hands in the form of a cross."

Since 1968, the Virgin Mary has appeared in Zeitoun, in suburban Cairo (Egypt), at least three times. She was accompanied by Joseph and Jesus, who in one vision was twelve years old. The other two times, the Holy Family appeared as shown on the images of their stay in Egypt—that is to say, with the Virgin Mary on a donkey's back and Joseph holding a rod—according to a witness.

Miracles Attributed to Joseph

We will see the story of thirty-one "miraculous examples that confirm St. Joseph's powerful credibility with God." They were published by Fr. Enfantin in *The Month of St. Joseph* in 1838.

The residents of Avignon's devotion to Joseph grew after

a miracle that occurred during the construction of the convent of their city's Discalced Carmelites. A mason fell while holding on to a rock. A Carmelite then prayed: "Oh, St. Joseph, quick, rescue him!" The young man fell on a pile of rocks. The one he was carrying fell on his chest. He got up without being hurt.

A morally corrupt Venetian man noticed an image of Joseph that was carved on a wall. He resolved to honor him every day. By being faithful to this resolution, he was really sorry for his sins after a while. He confessed them and died reconciled with God.

In 1631, a crater opened up on Mount Vesuvius, from which lava escaped and devastated the vicinity, including the place known as the Greek Man's Tower. Camille was here with his nephew, who was five years old. She called on Joseph while seeing her nephew being surrounded by lava. The saint saved the child by taking his hand.

Sr. Jeanne Rodriguez, from the Third Order of St. Francis, while traveling with a friend, was caught in a storm. A young man came to pull them out of it. This was Joseph—he spoke with them about the world's vanity and the invaluable price of God's grace and love.

José de Quiroga y Lozada (d. 1720) was a Spanish gentleman from Galicia. He surrendered the Mariana Islands to the king of Spain in 1699. During the fights against the natives, resorting to Joseph served as a shield for him. He gave him all the credit for his victories. One day, when he was attacked by a great number of opponents, who rained poisoned arrows down on his flock, he called on Joseph. The saint appeared in the air, and the Christian army saw him smash the arrows (*Story of the Mariana Islands*).

Joan of the Angels, who was already mentioned, became ill. Seeing that she was close to death, she very confidently called on Joseph, who miraculously and suddenly healed her.

ST. JOSEPH'S STAIRCASE

The mystery of St. Joseph's *Miracle of the Staircase* in Santa Fe, New Mexico, has endured for 140 years. It has attracted more than 250,000 visitors each year to the Loretto Chapel that was built by the Sisters of Loretto. The tradition says a miracle occurred there during the construction. The sisters noticed that the staircase to the choir loft had been forgotten. They then prayed a novena to Joseph, the patron saint of carpenters. On the last day of their prayer, a stranger knocked on their door. He introduced himself as a carpenter and offered to build the missing staircase all by himself. Nobody understood how the staircase could hold up without a central support post. The carpenter did not use a nail or glue. He mysteriously disappeared without being paid. Since then, people have been persuaded that this carpenter was Joseph himself, who was sent by Jesus Christ. The "miraculous staircase" and chapel have become a pilgrimage site.

PART VII

Praying

to

St. Joseph

Chronology of the Devotion to and Veneration of St. Joseph

Fifth century St. Joseph's birth is celebrated among the Copts.

Around **800** Rheinau's martyrology mentions a feast on March 19.

Around **1030** for the first time, the Feast of St. Joseph is celebrated in the Benedictine abbey in Winchester (a county in Hampshire in the United Kingdom).

1324 The Servites of Mary celebrate Joseph on March 19.

1476 Sixtus IV authorizes the Feast of St. Joseph to be on March 19 in Rome's breviary and Roman missal. At the request of the Friars Minor Conventual, he approves a Mass for Joseph with a simple rite.

1482 The Roman breviary organizes nine lessons for the Feast of St. Joseph.

1504 Proper votive Mass.

1567 This Mass is adopted by the Carthusian monks.

May 8, 1621 Gregory XV extends the liturgical feast and the Divine Office to the whole world.

1642 Urban VIII makes the feast mandatory.

1670 Clement X elevates the feast to a second-class rite.

April 6, 1680 Granting the Order of Carmel's requests, Innocent XI sets up the Feast of St. Joseph's Patronage for the Discalced Carmelites, with a proper office, on the third Sunday of Easter.

1690 First St. Joseph parish in Grenoble, France.

February 4, 1714 Clement XI gives the Feast of St. Joseph a proper of the Mass and the office.

December 19, 1726 Benedict XIII includes Joseph's name in the Litany of the Saints.

May 31, 1783 Pius VI approves the crowning of a miraculous canvas representing the Holy Family in the city of Kalisz (Poland), which attracts many pilgrims.

September 7, 1815 Pius VII authorizes the insertion of Joseph's name after the Virgin Mary's name in the *A Cunctis* prayer.

January 22, 1836 Gregory XVI grants particular indulgences to the faithful who practice the devotion of Joseph's Seven Sorrows and Seven Joys for the sick.

December 10, 1836 Pius IX extends the Feast of St. Joseph's Patronage to the third Sunday of Easter for the universal Church. It includes a second-class rite. Pius XII will move it to the following Wednesday.

February 1, 1847 Pius IX, in turn, grants indulgences for the same devotion.

1859 Pius IX approves the benediction of the cord of St. Joseph, whose devotion had spread in Belgium.

1865 Pius IX dedicates the month of March to St. Joseph, granting many graces and indulgences.

1869–1870 The council fathers of Vatican I give Pius IX a document that was signed by one hundred fifty-three bishops who ask for the veneration of Joseph to play a more important role in the holy liturgy. Another document, signed by forty-three superiors of religious orders, requests that Joseph be proclaimed the patron of the universal Church.

December 8, 1870 Pius IX proclaims Joseph as the patron of the universal Church, via the decree *Quemadmodum Deus.*

July 7, 1871 Pius IX publishes the apostolic letters *Inclytum Patriarcham*, in which he recalls all that his predecessors have done to promote the veneration of Joseph.

1878 Leo XIII, who was elected pope on February 20, places his pontificate under "the protection of St. Joseph, the heavenly patron of the Church."

1883 Leo XIII agrees to have Joseph's Mass and Divine Office every Wednesday.

August 15, 1889 *Quamquam Pluries*, an encyclical of Leo XIII, on Joseph's patronage.

1892 Some changes in the liturgical celebration of the Feast of St. Joseph are approved when it falls during the Passion and Holy Week.

1909 Pius X approves the litanies in honor of St. Joseph, enriching them with indulgences.

1911 The Sacred Congregation of Rites' July 11 *motu proprio* and July 24 *Urbi et Orbi* bring about some modifications to the feasts of St. Joseph and their liturgical ranks. The March 19 feast becomes the "Solemnity of St. Joseph, Spouse of the Blessed Virgin Mary, Confessor and Patron of the Universal Church."

1919 Benedict XV includes a proper preface for Joseph in the missal.

July 25, 1920 Benedict XV publishes the motu proprio *Bonum Sane et Salutare* and names Joseph as the efficacious advocate of the dying, while offering the Holy Family as a model for Christian homes.

1921 Benedict XV also includes St. Joseph's name in the popular *Bendito Sea Dios* prayer.

May 1, 1955 Pius XII announces and introduces the Feast of St. Joseph, craftsman and worker, with Mass and office propers and a text of the martyrology.

March 11, 1958 The Apostolic Penitentiary publishes the prayer of Pius XII to St. Joseph, which has extensive indulgences.

March 19, 1961 John XXIII's apostolic letter *Le Voci* encourages a devotion to Joseph.

1962 John XXIII puts Joseph's name in the Roman Canon of the Mass.

August 24, 1965 Canonical coronation of a statue of Joseph in St. Teresa of Ávila's first reformed convent.

August 15, 1989 John Paul II's apostolic exhortation *Redemptoris Custos*.

June 19, 2013 Pope Francis confirms the inclusion of Joseph's name in the Eucharistic prayers II, III, and IV of the third *editio typica* of the Roman missal, responding, in this way, to a desire of Benedict XVI.

It is not difficult to note that the devotion to Joseph was slow to take hold. The Jesuit Paul de Bary explained that God "wanted to overlook for six hundred years all the devotions that his servants had for the various saints, all the honors that were given them, and all the different ways of resorting to them for the deliverance of numerous ailments and for the confirmation of all kinds of holy desires. But all that was only to lead us to the devotion that we should have for this great saint that only came out in the time we are living in.[146] Pierre de Natali or Pierre Nadal (around 1330 to 1406) was the first one to include St. Joseph in his *Catalogus Sanctorum* on March 19.

TITLES OF ST. JOSEPH

He is considered a patriarch (from *arche*, "beginning" and *pater*, "father"). This is a title given to a man who we know is the father of many children. Through being married to Mary, he was the father of Christ, who, St. Paul told us, "brought many children to glory" (Heb. 2:10).

He is said to be a prophet, as Jesus' foster father, the head of the elect:

> Prophets have three attributes: first of all, better enlightenment, the interpretation of the Scriptures, and the manifestation of hidden things. The prophets had these three things, in a veiled light, in figures and enigmas. St. Joseph, who was enlightened by an angelic light, more clearly knew the great mystery of the Son of God, who was, similarly, the last prophet. After this mystery was revealed to him, he understood the most hidden meanings of the holy scriptures. He also cooperated in the mystery's manifestation in the whole world, after the time that divine wisdom scheduled it, by raising up the Son of God.[147]

He is all called the *great unknown* because of the silence around him. The hymn of Lauds says Joseph is "our life's sure hope," "the world's pillar," and the advocate of difficult causes.

Joseph in the Liturgical Calendar

Joseph is celebrated twice in the Catholic liturgical calendar—on March 19, his feast day, and on May 1 as the patron saint of laborers. There is also a votive Mass in honor of Joseph. A Mass in his honor was in a missal in the second half of the twelfth century, in the St. Florian convent in Lower Austria. It was entitled *De Sancto Joseph Nutriture Domini*.

The preface is the same for the three Masses and talks about Joseph's mission:

> It is truly right and just, our duty and our salvation, always and everywhere to give you thanks, Lord, holy Father, almighty and eternal God, and on the Solemnity of Saint Joseph to give you fitting praise, to glorify you and bless you. For this just man was given by you as spouse to the Virgin Mother of God and set as a wise and faithful servant in charge of your household to watch like a father over your Only Begotten Son, who was conceived by the overshadowing of the Holy Spirit, our Lord Jesus Christ. Through him the Angels praise your majesty, Dominions adore and Powers tremble before you. Heaven and the Virtues of heaven and the blessed Seraphim worship together with exultation. May our voices, we pray, join with theirs in humble praise, as we acclaim: Holy! . . . (Ordinary Form).
>
> It is truly just and necessary, our duty, and our salvation to give you thanks, holy Father, Eternal and Omnipotent God, and on the feast [of the solemnity, of the veneration] of blessed Joseph, to magnify you through the praises that you deserve, and to bless and celebrate you. He was a righteous man whom you gave as a spouse to the Virgin Mary,

the mother of God. He was a faithful and prudent servant who was established over your family, so that, standing in for a father, he would watch over your only Son, who was conceived in the mystery of the Holy Spirit. This is our Lord Jesus Christ, through whom the angels praise your majesty, the dominations adore you, the Powers revere you, and heaven and the powers of heaven, with the blessed Seraphim, united in joy, celebrate you. We ask you to let our voices be joined to their songs to proclaim in humble praise: Holy! . . . (Extraordinary Form).

Grant, we pray, almighty God, that by Saint Joseph's intercession your Church may constantly watch over the unfolding of the mysteries of human salvation, whose beginnings you entrusted to his faithful care. Through our Lord Jesus Christ, your Son, who lives and reigns with you in the unity of the Holy Spirit, one God, for ever and ever (Collect, March 19).

We pray, O Lord, that, just as Saint Joseph served with loving care your Only Begotten Son, born of the Virgin Mary, so we may be worthy to minister with a pure heart at your altar. Through Christ our Lord (Prayer over the Offerings, March 19).

Defend with unfailing protection, O Lord, we pray, the family you have nourished with food from this altar, as they rejoice at the Solemnity of Saint Joseph, and graciously keep safe your gifts among them. Through Christ our Lord (Prayer after Communion, March 19).

O God, Creator of all things, who laid down for the human race the law of work, graciously grant that by the example of Saint Joseph and under his patronage we may complete the works you set us to do and attain the rewards you promise. Through our Lord Jesus Christ, your Son, who lives and reigns with you in the unity of the Holy Spirit, one God, for ever and ever (Collect, May 1).

O God, fount of all mercy, look upon our offerings, which we bring before your majesty in commemoration of Saint Joseph, and mercifully grant that the gifts we offer may become the means of protection for those who call upon you. Through Christ our Lord. (Prayer over the Offerings, May 1).

Having fed upon heavenly delights, we humbly ask you, O Lord, that, by Saint Joseph's example, cherishing in our hearts the signs of your love, we may ever enjoy the fruit of perpetual peace. Through Christ our Lord. (Prayer after Communion, May 1).

O God, who in your inexpressible providence were pleased to choose Saint Joseph as spouse of the most holy mother of your Son, grant, we pray, that we, who revere him as our protector on earth, may be worthy of his heavenly intercession. Through our Lord Jesus Christ, your Son, who lives and reigns with you in the unity of the Holy Spirit, one God, for ever and ever (Collect, Votive Mass of St. Joseph).

As we prepare to offer the sacrifice of praise, O holy Father, we humbly ask to be sustained in our service by the prayers of Saint Joseph, whom you called to watch like a father on earth over your Only Begotten Son. Who lives and reigns for ever and ever (Prayer over the Offerings, Votive Mass of St. Joseph).

Restored by these life-giving sacraments, Lord, may we live for you always in justice and holiness, helped by the example and intercession of Saint Joseph, who in carrying out your great mysteries served you as a man just and obedient. Through

Christ our Lord (Prayer after Communion, Votive Mass of St. Joseph).

HYMNS IN HONOR OF ST. JOSEPH

Te Joseph Celebrant, hymn attributed to Pope Clement XI (1700-1721):

To you, Joseph, the hosts of heaven,
And the united, vibrant choir of Christendom
To you, great saint, who effect a chaste marriage
To the most glorious virgin.

When you saw your betrothed great with sacred fruit,
Amazement and doubt troubled your heart.
But the angel taught you that the infant was conceived
By the breath of the Holy Spirit.

Your hands swaddled the newborn Lord,
Your steps followed his flight into far-off Egypt,
Him lost in Jerusalem, sought, found,
You shed tears of joy.
After death most are blest by a loving destiny,
And, when they have won the palm, they are welcomed into glory.
But you, while you lived, like the saints above, were with God,
Blest more than others by this wondrous lot.

Spare us, sovereign Trinity, as we pray,
Grant that through Joseph's merits we may rise to heaven,

So that at last we may forever sing
The hymn of honor.

This hymn is recited or sung for the vespers of the solemnity of St. Joseph and for the Feast of St. Joseph the Worker.

Laeto cantu, sequence for the vespers in honor of St. Joseph (Extraordinary Form):

Let us exalt the spouse of the chaste Virgin Mary by joyfully singing.
Let us praise the foster father of an incarnate God.
Oh, what a noble charge the Father has entrusted to you!
Happy the one to whom the virgin mother submits herself as a wife:
What great duties you perform, head of the Holy Family!
Provide for a God's childhood with so much care!
The king whom the elements obey submits to you.
The one who is under your leadership maintains the earth's foundations.
Your obedience has no deadline. You lead the child with the Virgin Mary
to Egypt's borders.
Your life is consumed between the Savior's arms, not so much through the cross as through the eyes of love.
What light you enjoy! How high is the throne where you exalt your adopted son.
O, you who were given to Christ as a father, make him favor us,
And may your spouse, the virgin, also favor her children. Amen.

The Mass and St. Joseph

It is possible to bring out some titles that Joseph helps us with at the beginning of the celebration of the Holy Mass. 1) If Mary is spiritually present at the altar with the unique title of co-redemptrix, Joseph is her spouse. Jesus, the Redeemer, is the fruit of their marriage. 2) Jesus very sincerely named Joseph his father. Joseph loved Jesus as a real father and nourished him. He is the one who, with Mary, "prepared" the sovereign priest and divine victim of the upcoming sacrifice of the Passion.[148]) Mary and Joseph are an integral part of the devotion of Christians, just like in the plan of the redeeming Incarnation. 4) The sacrifice is offered by the whole Church and for the whole Church at Mass.

So if Mary is the mother of the Church, Joseph was designated to be its father. Eucharistic Prayer 1 proclaims that "in communion with those whose memory we venerate, especially the glorious ever-virgin Mary, mother of our God and Lord, Jesus Christ, and blessed Joseph, her spouse," etc. 6) Mary is our mediatrix who enables us to come to Jesus, the unique mediator before the Father. Joseph, the head of the Holy Family, introduces us to the mediatrix.3

PRAYER TO ST. JOSEPH BEFORE MASS

O blessed Joseph, happy man, to whom it was given not only to see and to hear that God whom many kings longed to see, and saw not, to hear, and heard not; but also to carry him in your arms, to embrace him, to clothe him, and guard and defend him.

Pray for us, O blessed Joseph.

That we may be made worthy of the promises of Christ.

Let us pray. O God, who has given us a royal priesthood, we beseech thee, that as blessed Joseph was found worthy to touch with his hands, and to bear in his arms, thy only-begotten Son, born of the Virgin Mary, so may we be made fit by cleanness of heart and blamelessness of life, to minister at thy holy altar; may we, this day, with reverent devotion partake of the sacred Body and Blood of your only-begotten Son, and may we in the world to come be accounted worthy of receiving an everlasting reward. Through the same Christ our Lord. Amen.

PRAYER TO ST. JOSEPH AFTER MASS

O Guardian of virgins and father, St. Joseph, to whose faithful custody innocence itself, Christ Jesus, and Mary, virgin of virgins, was committed; I pray and beseech thee by each of these dear pledges, Jesus and Mary, that, being preserved from all uncleanness, I may with spotless mind, pure heart, and a chaste body ever serve Jesus and Mary most chastely all the days of my life. Amen.

Veneration of Joseph's Heart

The devotion to the hearts of Jesus, Mary, and Joseph appeared in Portugal and Brazil in 1733. Then, the devotion to the Heart of St. Joseph flourished in Mexico in the eighteenth and nineteenth centuries. Having been approved by Pope Gregory XVI, Fr. Eli of the Three Hearts, who was a Discalced Carmelite, began traveling to France and Italy in 1843 to promote the devotion to Joseph's "righteous and most humble" heart. Fr. Michele Bocca, an oblate of Mary, founded the Pious Union of the Most Pure Heart of Joseph in 1846. Some literature that spread the devotion to the heart of Joseph emerged in the nineteenth century.

However, during an audience that was granted to the president of the Pious Union on September 18, 1873, Pope Pius IX asserted that this devotion was an abuse and had not been approved by the Church.

Yet the recent Magisterium, especially St. John Paul II's, spoke clearly about the heart of Joseph, without taking a stand on the subject: "The mystery of the divine incarnation! It was so difficult to understand that it must first be received in the mind and heart of human beings—above all, in the heart of Mary, which occurred with the Annunciation in Nazareth, and then in the heart of Joseph, Mary's spouse."[149]

ST. JOSEPH SCAPULAR

This scapular's devotion owes its origin not to revelations or miracles, but, first and foremost, to the Confraternity of the Cord in Verona in 1865. Its members wore a scapular as a sign of devotion to Joseph as a protector of the Church and the Roman pontiff (the loss of the Papal States and the occupation of Rome occurred in 1870)—and even more to Mère Marie de la Croix, a Franciscan tertiary. She was the founder and superior general of the Franciscan Sisters of the Immaculate Conception of Lons-le-Saunier (Jura), who was helped by a priest named Fr. Pierre-Baptiste, a Capuchin from Reims. The nun started to wear the scapular in 1876. At her request, the Capuchin made the design. Leo XIII approved the scapular in 1893. He entrusted its distribution to the Capuchin Friars Minor. The scapular was made by some Clarist sisters. Its three colors convey Joseph's three main virtues. Purple stands for his humility, gold or yellow his justice, and white his purity.

Patron of a Happy Death

The Church has always venerated Joseph for preparing himself to die while fully trusting God. Tradition, in fact, shows him as being completely peaceful when he died and surrounded by the affection of Jesus and Mary. He appears like this on a bas-relief in front of the altar dedicated to our Lord's holy agony in the Lazarists' home in Paris. On the first Friday of the month, quite a few members of the archconfraternity meet there. Among the reasons to call on Joseph at the moment of death are a) "Joseph is the father of our Judge, whose other saints are only friends. b) his power is more astounding for demons. c) his death is the most privileged and gentlest one that ever existed."[150]

St. Alphonsus Maria de Liguori also gave three reasons for this devotion:

> The first is that Jesus Christ loved him, not only as his friend, but also as his father. This makes his intercession much more powerful than that of the other saints. . . . The second reason is that St. Joseph has more power over the demons that attack us at the end of our lives. The Lord gave him the very

special privilege of protecting the dying against Lucifer's traps, as a reward for having saved him from Herod's traps. Finally, the third reason is that St. Joseph, because of the help that he got from Jesus and Mary when he was dying, enjoys the privilege of securing a holy and gentle death for his servants. If they call on him in their last moments, he will come to strengthen them through his visit and provide them, in addition, with the help of Jesus and Mary (*Devotion to St. Joseph*).[151]

The litanies of St. Joseph call on him as the "hope of the sick, the support for the dying, and the terror of demons." Indeed, he can teach us to die serenely, with the peace of heart that expresses one's love for God to the end.

On February 17, 1913, Pope Pius X built the international center of the Pious Union of St. Joseph for the Salvation of the Dying, under Joseph's patronage. On September 15, 1919, Card. Mercier, the archbishop of Malines and the primate of Belgium, canonically built a national center of this association in the abbey of the Postel Norbertines. On December 12, 1940, a center for this association was also built for southern Belgium by the bishop of Namur in the Norbertine church of Our Lady of Leffe Abbey near Dinant. The goal of this apostolate is to gather priests, nuns, and faithful laypeople in a charitable organization to help the many people who are dying every day through Masses, Communions, sacrifices, and good works. A confraternity for a good death, under Joseph's patronage, was built in 1648, in the Jesuit church in Rome—the *Gesù*. It is the main confraternity for a good death. The one that was built in the church in Montréjeau (Haute-Garonne) was affiliated with it in 1859.

MEMORARE TO ST. JOSEPH

It is the counterpart of the *Memorare*, which was addressed to the Blessed Virgin Mary and attributed to St. Bernard. "Remember, O most pure spouse of the Virgin Mary, my beloved patron, that never has it been heard that anyone invoked your patronage and sought your aid without being comforted. Inspired by this confidence, I come to you and fervently commend myself to you. Despise not my petition, O dearest foster father of our Redeemer, but accept it graciously" (invested with an indulgence by Pope Pius IX in 1863).

Patron of the Universal Church

At the urgent request of the fathers of the First Vatican Council, Pope Pius IX declared Joseph's patronage over the universal Church on December 8, 1870. His patronage was confirmed by Leo XIII, in the encyclical *Quamquam Pluries*, on August 15, 1889.

> Jesus Christ, for the glory of his own name, destined St. Joseph to be the patron of the Church Militant's entire empire. This is why, before Judgment Day, all people will know, venerate, and adore the Lord's name and the magnificent gifts that God gave St. Joseph. These are gifts that he wanted to leave almost hidden for such a long period of time.[152]

He is the patron of youth educators, the interior life, and the Christian family.

ST. FRANCIS DE SALES AND ST. JOSEPH

Francis de Sales (1567-1622) is a perfect model of devotion to St. Joseph. Fr. Faber said that "God raised him up to teach [that devotion] and spread it among the people." He loved and venerated him more than anyone. Joseph "could make angels envious and defy all of heaven to have more goods than he did. Who is there among the angels who is comparable to the queen of Angels, and in God, more than God?"[153]

He was dedicated to him very early on and tried his hardest all his life to serve and glorify him. He called him "the glorious father of our Savior and our first love, his first admirer, along with Mary, the husband of the world's queen, the accomplished model of all virtues, and the epitome of virginity, modesty, humility, and steadfastness." A dedicatory prayer opens the *Treatise on the Love of God*:

Glorious St. Joseph, Mary's spouse, give us, we beg you, your paternal protection through Jesus Christ's heart.

O you whose power extends to all needs and knows how to make the most impossible things possible for us, open your fatherly eyes to your children's interests. In the difficulty and pain that press us, we confidently resort to you. Please charitably guide this important and difficult matter, which is causing our anxiety. Make its favorable outcome turn to God's glory and the benefit of his servants. Amen! . . .

O great St. Joseph, very beloved spouse of the beloved Mary! Hey! How many times you have taken the love of heaven and earth between your arms! While ablaze with this divine child's embraces and kisses, your soul easily melted when he tenderly said in your arms (O God, what sweetness!) that you were his great friend and very dear beloved father! In the past, people put lamps of the former temple on golden lilies. O peerless Mary and Joseph, sacred lilies of incomparable beauty, between whom the beloved enjoys himself and delights all his lovers!

The nineteenth of the *True Spiritual Conferences* is completely dedicated to Joseph:

O what a saint the glorious St. Joseph is! . . . Notwithstanding who he was, he lived in a state of great poverty and abjectness for his whole life—a poverty and abjectness under which he kept his great virtues and dignity hidden and covered. But my God, what dignity! To be our Lord's tutor, and not only that, but his putative father and his most holy mother's spouse! . . . There is no doubt, my dear sisters, that St. Joseph was braver than David and wiser than Solomon. And how wise he was, since God put him in charge of his most glorious Son and was chosen to be his tutor. . . .

There is no doubt that St. Joseph was gifted with all the graces and gifts that warranted the task that God wanted to give him related to the temporal and domestic economy of our Lord Jesus and the management of his family. It was composed of only three people, which represents the mystery of the most holy and adorable Trinity. Mary, Jesus, and Joseph were a marvelously commendable trinity that was worthy to be honored."

Francis de Sales dedicated the Order of the Visitation's first church to Joseph. He had it built in Annecy and gave Joseph to the order as their patron and father. Among Joseph's virtues, Francis stressed his perfect humility, his sense of unworthiness, acceptance of material poverty, total submission to God's will, and perseverance in trial. Francis de Sales indicated that, like the palm tree, Joseph "hid his flowers, that is to say, his virtues, under the veil of the most holy humility up to the time of his death." He spent his whole life in poverty and "abjectness," despite his greatness before God. Francis also presented Joseph as the model of perseverance.

Finally, we note, in the same saint, a perfect obedience as well as bravery and strength that make him triumph over the devil and the world. Francis de Sales thought Joseph was in the glory of heaven in body and soul.[154]

Sanctuaries

In the sixteenth century, Isidore of Isolanis predicted that "before Judgment Day, everyone will know, venerate, and adore the Lord's name. They will proclaim the blessings that God has guaranteed us in St. Joseph, and that he wanted kept hidden for a long time. This is why Joseph's name will be a guarantee of many blessings. We will build temples and celebrate feasts in his honor. For the Lord will open the faithful's ears of understanding, and famous men will scrutinize the interior gifts that God hid in St. Joseph. There, they will find a splendid treasure, such as the holy fathers in the Old Testament did not find. All of this will occur particularly through an effect of the light of the holy angels."

In Puy-en-Velay (Haute-Loire), a huge statue of Joseph holding the baby Jesus was placed at the top of a rock sixty meters high. A grotto is in the rock. There is a sanctuary at its side that, today, is run by three priests from the Community of St. Martin. The sanctuary's grace is the grace of "inner healing."

The most important sanctuary and pilgrimage site in the world dedicated to Joseph is in Montreal (in the province of Quebec, Canada). It is St. Joseph's Oratory of Mount Royal.

Originally, it was a chapel that was 155 meters high, built on Mount Royal in 1904 on Br. André's initiative. The construction of the current building started in 1924 and ended in 1967. Its dome is sixty meters high, with a diameter of thirty-nine meters. The cross at the top overlooks the city by 300 meters. It is the third biggest church in the world after St. Peter's Basilica in Rome and the Basilica of Our Lady of Peace in Yamoussoukro (Ivory Coast).

Many crutches, canes, girdles, and protheses that were left *ex voto* by the sick who were healed at the oratory line the walls of a votive chapel that was built for this purpose.

A life-size Way of the Cross was unveiled in 1951 in the adjacent gardens. It includes forty-two people placed in sixteen stations. An impressive monument to Joseph carrying the child Jesus in his arms was unveiled in 1923. The inscription "Ite ad Joseph" appears on the base. The oratory's museum includes more than 900 mangers coming from all over the world.

The oratory, which was built as a basilica in 1955, attracts more than two million people per year. St. John Paul II came to pray there in 1984.

ST. JOSEPH'S RELICS

In the absence of *ex corpore* relics, since a devout belief asserts that Joseph was taken up to heaven (see chapter 1), the *ex indumenta* relics, or venerated clothes, are, first of all, the coat with which he wrapped the infant Jesus when he was born and his shoes. In the nineteenth century, the Crusaders brought back various relics from the Holy Land—rings, rods, belts, coats, etc.

Wedding ring. According to Benedict XIV, the ring with which Joseph married the Blessed Virgin Mary, following a devout belief, is being kept in Perouse (in the cathedral). The *Compagnia del Santo Anello e San Giuseppe* was founded in 1487 to ensure its safekeeping. It ordered an altar painting for the St. Joseph chapel in the cathedral in Pinturrichio, and then in Capoali. It bailed out. In the end, Perugin created it. But churches in Semur-en-Auxois; Burgundy; and Siena, Italy claimed this same relic.

Rod. The city of Florence has kept Joseph's rod that miraculously flowered in the Temple of Jerusalem when he married Mary. The flowers in question are depicted as white, customarily lilies, to signify Joseph's virginity. They can be replaced by leaves. The rod can be used to carry a bundle or gourd. Fragments of the rod are kept in the church known as Santa Cecilia in Trastavere in Rome as well as in the collegiate church in Ariccia and the cathedral in Anagni. A miracle-working travel rod is kept in Annecy (Haute-Savoie).

Belt. It was returned from a crusade, around 1248, by Jean de Joinville, at the end of the first of St. Louis's crusades. He had it placed in a chapel that was built *ex professo*, and in which he had himself buried, with the following inscription: "Nos Zona sancti Josephi e Terra Sancta asportata ab eo feliciter donati, etc." Richelieu and Louis XIII came to venerate it. It is in a reliquary, dating from 1868, in Notre-Dame in Joinville (Haute-Marne).

Shoes. It has been said that they were kept in Aix-la-Chapelle. They were cut out at the Virgin Mary's request and were used to warm the Child Jesus in the absence of swaddling clothes. In the second half of the fourteenth century, iconography, the theater, and popular songs took up the subject (Payan). Bigger slippers are kept in the abbey St. Symeon of Trier.

Shirt. A piece of it is displayed courtesy of the Franciscans at Castel Gandolfo.

Han. This is the sound that comes out of a man's chest when he splits wood. One of Joseph's *hans* was being kept in a bottle, in Courchiverny, near Blois.

Coat. Some pieces of it are found in churches in Rome—Chiesa Nuova, St. Mary Major, St. Pudentiana, San Marco, Santa Susanna, Holy Apostles, San Lorenzo in Lucina, San Silvestre a Monte Cavallo, Santa Anastasia in Palatino, Santa Maria Regina Coeli alla Lungara, and outside Rome, in the collegiate church in Ariccia, the one in Marino, the Agnani cathedral, and the parish church in Castel Gandolfo. A coat is also in Toledo.

Bones. The Camaldolese in Tusculum have "Joseph's bones." There is room for doubt about their authenticity for the above reason.

Pallium. A canon in Digne brought over a piece for the St. Joseph chapel in La Pérusse.

Clothes. The Roman church Santa Cecilia in Trastevere has some, along with the Passionists in Monte Calvi and the

Franciscans in Frascati. In 1141, during the creation of St. Pétrone in the Santo Stefano church in Bologna, some *reliquiae sancti Joseph* were discovered, which testifies to a devotion given to the saint in Bologna, to say the least.

Litanies of St. Joseph

Joseph's name has always appeared in litanies for the counsel of the soul, as well as in specific liturgies of the Dominicans and Carmelites. On the other hand, he disappeared from major litanies during the reform of the Breviary when Pius V was pope. During Clement XI's pontificate, the Congregation of Rites received many requests to have it re-established, but with no result. The German emperor, the grand duke of Tuscany, the Electoral Palace, the Electorate of Cologne, other sovereigns, and forty procurators general of religious orders revisited the task. Nonetheless, people had to wait for a decree in 1726, under Benedict XIII, for this request to be granted and for the name to be re-established, after John the Baptist's name.

There are many versions of litanies specific to Joseph. We will end with one of them:

Lord, have mercy on us [2x].
Christ, have mercy on us [2x].
Lord, have mercy on us. Christ, hear us (2x).
Christ, graciously hear us.
God the Father of Heaven,
Have mercy on us.
God the Son, Redeemer of the world,
Have mercy on us.
God the Holy Spirit,
Have mercy on us.

Holy Trinity, one God,
Have mercy on us.
Holy Mary, pray for us.
St. Joseph, pray for us.
Light of the patriarchs, pray for us.
Spouse of the mother of God, pray for us.
Chaste guardian of the virgin, pray for us.
Foster father of the Son of God, pray for us.
Watchful defender of Christ, pray for us.
Head of the Holy Family, pray for us.
Joseph most just, pray for us.
Joseph most chaste, pray for us.
Joseph most prudent, pray for us.
Joseph most valiant, pray for us.
Joseph most obedient, pray for us.
Joseph most faithful, pray for us.
Mirror of patience, pray for us.
Lover of poverty, pray for us.
Model of workmen, pray for us.
Glory of domestic life, pray for us.
Guardian of virgins, pray for us.
Pillar of families, pray for us.
Solace of the afflicted, pray for us.
Hope of the sick, pray for us.
Patron of the dying, pray for us.
Terror of demons, pray for us.
Protector of Holy Church, pray for us.

Lamb of God, who takes away the sins of the world,
Spare us, O Lord.
Lamb of God, who takes away the sins of the world,
Graciously hear us, O Lord.
Lamb of God, who takes away the sins of the world,
Have mercy on us.

V. He made him the lord of his household.
R. And prince over all his possessions.

Let us pray.

O God, who in your ineffable providence were pleased to choose blessed Joseph to be the spouse of your most holy mother, grant that as we venerate him as our protector on earth, we may be worthy to have him as our intercessor in heaven, you who live and reign forever and ever. Amen.

Endnotes

1 An administrative region in southeastern France.

2 Nineteenth-century French abbot and writer.

3 St. Josemaría, *When Christ Goes By.*

4 Bertrand Martelet, twentieth-century French priest and writer.

5 St. Bernard, *Homily 2 on Missus Est*, 16.

6 Twentieth-century French priest and scholar.

7 Epistle to the Ephesians 19:1.

8 This and other citations from the above section from *Summa Theologiae* (ST) III q.29 a.1 co.

9 *Commentary on St. Matthew* 1:20.

10 *Against Heresies* 3, 21, 6-7.

11 ST III q.28 a.3 r.2.

12 ST III q.29 a.2 co.

13 Seventeenth-century French bishop and preacher.

14 Second Homily on the Glories of Mary 12.

15 Irenaeus, *Against Heresies* 3, 22, 4.

16 F.M. William, *The Life of Mary, Mother of Jesus.*

17 *Allocution*, March 19, 1969. Quoted in the John Paul II exhortation *Redemptoris Custos*, no. 26.

18 Antonin Sertillanges, French Dominican philosopher in the late nineteenth and early twentieth centuries.

19 French theologian and author, 1849-1927.

20 Sermon 291, 5.

21 *Revelations*.

22 Homily 4 on the Gospel of Matthew.

23 *Ibid*.

24 Sermon 51.

25 Commentary on the *Diatesseron*.

26 Commentary on the Gospel of St. Matthew.

27 Homily 4 on St. Matthew.

28 A fifteenth-century Passion play.

29 *On the Flesh of Christ* 21.

30 French Jesuit priest and scholar in the late nineteenth and early twentieth centuries.

31 Augustine, *Sermon* 51, 20, 30; PL 38, 350-351.

32 Homilies on Leviticus 12.

33 Cited by St. Alphonsus Liguori, Sermon for the Feast of St. Joseph.

34 Twentieth-century French Benedictine and scholar.

35 Sermon 51, 16, 26.

36 *Compendium Theologicæ Veritatis*.

37 Letter 586.

38 Homily on the Gospel of Matthew 14.

39 Canon Leon Cristiani, twentieth-century French theologian.

40 St. Alphonsus Liguori, *Exhortations to Lead Souls toward a Devotion to St. Joseph*, fifth meditation.

41 *Summa de Donis Santci Joseph*.

42 Paul Claudel, twentieth-century French poet.

43 Servant of God Romano Guardini, twentieth-century Italian-German priest and scholar.

44 Commentary on St. Matthew 2:12.

45 Commentary on St. Matthew 2:21.

46 Homily *Super Missus Est*.

47 *Homilia I Super Missus Est*, 7

48 *Exhortations to Lead Souls toward a Devotion to St. Joseph*, seventh meditation.

49 *Homily IV in Matthaeum, 3.*

50 *Revelations* 7:25.

51 Letter to Sylvain Pitt, March 24, 1901.

52 Twentieth-century French Scripture scholar.

53 Pope Francis, Homily for the Inaugural Mass of His Pontificate, March 19, 2013.

54 Marie-Bernard d'Alès, French contemplative priest and former exorcist.

55 Nineteenth-century Italian Jesuit and author of a manual of devotion to St. Joseph.

56 *Meditation on the Death of St. Joseph.*

57 *A Manual of Practical Devotion to St. Joseph.*

58 Jean Charlier de Gerson, fifteenth-century French theologian.

59 *Saint Joseph, Spouse of the Holy Virgin,* by Alexis-Henri-Marie Lépicier, French cardinal in the early twentieth century.

60 *Discourse on St. Joseph, Spouse of the Holy Virgin.*

61 *Sermon for the Feast of St. Joseph 2.*

62 Sermon I on St. Joseph.

63 *Chart of St. Joseph's Prominent Qualities, 1629.*

64 Joaquin Ferrer Arrellano, contemporary Spanish theologian and priest of Opus Dei.

65 *Homilia super Missus Est* 2:16.

66 *In Hom. I in Genesis.*

67 St. Josemaría, *Christ Is Passing By.*

68 *Homilia II Super Missus est* 16.

69 *Pensées.*

70 *Against Heresies* 3, 21, 8.

71 *First Panegyric on St. Joseph* 3.

72 Early twentieth-century French theological writer.

73 *Meeting with Families*, Manila, January 16, 2015.

74 Abbé Albert Michel, twentieth-century French priest and scholar; "St. Joseph," *Dictionnaire de Théologie Catholique.*

75 Abbé Albert Michel, "St. Joseph," *Dictionnaire de Théologie Catholique.*

76 St. Alphonsus Liguori, *Exhortations to Lead Souls to Devotion Toward St. Joseph*, seventh meditation.

77 St. Alphonsus Liguori, *Sermon for the Feast of St. Joseph* 2.

78 John Paul II, June 18, 1996.

79 *Sermo de Nativitate Virginis Mariae.*

80 Dom Gérard, *Joseph's Greatness.*

81 Dom Démaret, *Mary from Whom Jesus Was Born.*

82 *De Sancto Joseph* 3:2.

83 Louis Cardinal Billot (1846-1931), French Jesuit priest and theologian.

84 Abbé Albert Michel, "St. Joseph," *Dictionnaire de Théologie Catholique.*

85 *Against Helvidius.*

86 John Paul II, August 21, 1996.

87 de Liguori, Alphonsus Maria. *Exhortations to Lead Souls to a Devotion to Saint Joseph.*

88 Bernardine of Siena, Sermon on "Joseph, Faithful Guardian."

89 Dom Marechaux, *Elevations About St. Joseph.*

90 A. Doze, *Discovering St. Joseph.*

91 Henri-Marie Manteau-Bonamy, twentieth-century French theological writer.

92 *Homilia II Super Missus Est.*

93 *Sermon I of St. Joseph.*

94 *Summa de Doni Danctis Joseph.*

95 ST II-II q.182 a.1, ad 3.

96 Claude Quinard, *St. Joseph*.

97 *A Manual of Practical Devotion to St. Joseph*.

98 Bernardine of Siena, *Sermon About St. Joseph*.

99 *Evangelical Preparation* 7:3.

100 Paul VI, *Homily*, March 19, 1968.

101 St. Francis de Sales, Twentieth Sermon on St. Joseph.

102 Jean Richard, *Elogios Historicos de los Santos* (1780).

103 Gioacchino Ventura di Raulica. *Encyclopédie de la Prédication Contemporaine, Homélies sur les Paraboles de N.-S. Jésus-Christ*. J. Mingardon: Marseille, 1880, p. 330.

104 Michel Gasnier, twentieth-century Dominican and author of *The Silences of St. Joseph*.

105 Card. Lepicier, *Saint Joseph: Spouse of the Holy Virgin*.

106 *Ibid.*

107 Charles-René Billuart, *Panegyric on St. Joseph*, 1830.

108 Thomas Aquinas, *Super Matthaeum*.

109 Alphonsus de Liguori. *Oeuvres Complètes* (Béthune et Plon: Paris, 1935), bk. 6, p. 511.

110 Fr. Jean Jacquinot, *The Glory of St. Joseph*.

111 Fr. Denis Buzy, nineteenth-century French priest and archeologist.

112 Abbot Barthélemy-Llouis Enfantin, *The Month of St. Joseph*.

113 Bossuet, *Second Panegyric on St. Joseph*.

114 *Ibid.*

115 *Bethlehem.*

116 Twentieth-century French Carmelite priest and writer.

117 Augustine, Sermon 51.

118 Bossuet, *First Panegyric on St. Joseph*.

119 Hardon, John A. "St. Joseph: Foster Father of Jesus" (Inter Mirifica, 1999).

120 Pius XII, *Superiore anno.*

121 Bossuet, *Second Panegyric on St. Joseph.*

122 Ibid.

123 *Social Science*, March 1909.

124 Twentieth-century French Dominican and author of *St. Joseph the Silent.*

125 Fourteenth-century French cardinal and theologian.

126 *The Twelve Glories of St. Joseph.*

127 Escrivá, Josemaría. *When Christ Goes By.*

128 John Paul II, Homily, March 19, 1983.

129 St. Alphonsus Liguori. *Exhortations to Carry Souls to a Devotion to St. Joseph*, seventh meditation.

130 Contemporary French writer.

131 St. Josémaría Escrivá, *The Forge.*

132 Thirteenth-century French Franciscan.

133 Paul Payan, *An Image of Fatherhood in the Medieval West.*

134 *Devotion to St. Joseph.*

135 Isidore of Isolanis, *Saint Joseph*, 3:18

136 See Joseph Perrin, *A Just Man Named Joseph.*

137 John Paul II, Homily, September 9, 1993.

138 Patrignani, *A Manual of Practical Devotion to St. Joseph.*

139 Alphonsus de Liguori, *Devotion to St. Joseph.*

140 Isolani, Isidoro. *Summa de donis sancti Ioseph* 3:6.

141 Francis de Sales, Letter to St. Jane Frances de Chantal. March 17, 1661.

142 Francis de Sales, "Virtues of St. Joseph," 19.

143 *The Incalculable Treasure of St. Joseph,* 1645.

144 Prayer composed by St. John Eudes.

145 *The Twelve Stars of St. Joseph.*

146 *Devotion to St. Joseph.*

147 Isidore of Isolanis, *Saint Joseph, 3:18*

148 See Joseph Perrin, *A Just Man Named Joseph.*

149 John Paul II, Homily, September 9, 1993.

150 Patrignani, *A Manual of Practical Devotion to St. Joseph.*

151 Alphonsus de Liguori, *Devotion to St. Joseph.*

152 Isolani, Isidoro. *Summa de donis sancti Ioseph 3:6.*

153 Francis de Sales, Letter to St. Jane Frances de Chantal. March 17, 1661.

154 Francis de Sales, "Virtues of St. Joseph," 19.